BREAK INTO THE SCENE

A Musician's Guide to
Making Connections
Creating Opportunities
and Launching a Career

Seth Hanes

Praise for *Break into the Scene*

"*Break Into the Scene* gets right to the point - a successful musician is more than a top-notch performer. Seth's book is an efficient, entertaining guide to all of the tools necessary to create your musical career."

– Paul Bryan, Dean of Students and
Faculty at Curtis Institute of Music

"*Break into the Scene* is a terrific, straight-talking, and down to earth guide for freelance success. Loaded with practical advice and examples, the book uncovers the mind traps and misperceptions that prevent musicians from succeeding—and Seth offers real-life solutions!"

– Angela Beeching, author of *Beyond Talent*

"As someone who has struggled with an irrational fear of networking and gigging, I'm so relieved that Seth has taken on the impressive feat of dissecting the art of music freelancing into an inspiring set of mindsets, mantras, and steps that anyone can take. If you're interesting in freelancing as a musician, this book is the first place you should start."

– Rob Knopper, MET Orchestra percussionist and
founder of auditionhacker

"I was a hardcore freelancer for many years and Seth's advice for getting into the business is priceless. It's not being in the right place at the right time, It's being somewhere all the time. Every musician needs to know exactly what works in the freelance world and Seth's plain truths will get you gigs!"

– Jeffrey Lang, Associate-Principal Horn,
The Philadelphia Orchestra

"This book is a treasure trove of valuable and practical advice for all aspiring musicians."

– Michael Krajewski, Music Director of The Philly Pops and Principal Pops Conductor of the Houston, Atlanta and Jacksonville Symphonies

"If I were going to recommend one book to anyone getting started in the music business, this is it."

– Frank Giordano, President and CEO of
The Philly POPS

"With his new book, Seth hits directly at the important matters for everyone, whether you're breaking into the scene or already in it. We must be especially positive, proactive, aware of our behavior and most of all, easy to work with. Not surprisingly, Seth is all of these things. Bravo!"

– Eric Reed, American Brass Quintet and The Juilliard School faculty member

"If you're a musician who's struggling to get your career off the ground, do yourself a favor and read this book."

> – Charlie Hoehn, author of *Play it Away* and
> *Recession-Proof Graduate*, entrepreneur, and speaker

"This book is game-changer for any creative freelancer."

> – David Kadavy, author of *Design for Hackers* and host
> of the Love Your Work podcast

FREE BONUSES

As a thank you for checking out my book, I have put together a set of totally free bonuses including PDF versions of the exact email templates that you can use to start getting more gigs today.

One reader landed a $1,200 gig using just one of these email templates.

visit breakintothescene.com/bonuses

TABLE OF CONTENTS

INTRODUCTION

I felt absolutely lost.

How in the world was I going to make a career in music?

I finished school and did everything I was told.

I went to so many rehearsals I lost count.

I practiced relentlessly for my lessons, and I studied for my classes.

But after all of this, the thought of venturing out into *the real world* as a musician was horrifying.

At the time, it didn't exactly feel like I had the ingredients for success.

I read all of the books and blogs, listened to the "experts," and even dug around on YouTube desperately hoping for some random video that might help point me in the right direction.

After doing all of this research, one thing became frustratingly clear.

There is a plethora of information about *what's possible* but not enough with actionable advice about *how to actually do it*.

This book is my response to that.

What makes this book different

When I set out to write this book, my goal was to fill it with actionable advice that anyone can implement, no matter where they are in their career.

At some point, we've all gotten excited about an idea but had no clue how to make it a reality.

For me, that's how I felt about getting started as a freelancer.

I was eager to begin, but clueless how to make it happen.

Maybe you've felt the same way.

This book focuses on one thing, and one thing only: how to take the first steps to launch your freelance music career.

Not every musician wants to do freelance work, and that's all right.

I totally understand that.

Whether you are trying to freelance full-time, pick up a few private students, or just looking to supplement your income while taking auditions or working on other projects, this book will help you develop the skill set necessary to pursue as much or as little freelance work as you want.

The truth is, most people waste their time worrying about things that don't matter and end up accomplishing nothing.

I was plagued by this for months.

To help you learn from my mistakes, I will show you the things I wish I'd done differently, and the things that really helped get my career going.

This book is different from the others because it is based on the personal experience of someone who has built a career around freelance work.

The strategies and tactics outlined in this book will help point you in the right direction to get your career off the ground.

My story

When I finished college, the only things I had going for me were a handful of random gigs, a job in a parking garage, and daunting student loans.

These days, I am an active freelancer, contractor, and I run my own business as a digital marketing consultant and web designer.

I've had the pleasure of working with everyone from orchestral musicians in the Philadelphia Orchestra and the New York Philharmonic to multi-million dollar performing arts organizations.

This drastic career shift certainly didn't happen overnight.

Not long before this success, while still in music school, I was completely freaking out because I had no idea what I was going to do with my life after graduation.

About six months before graduation, I started reading every book I could get my hands on about marketing, business, and entrepreneurship, while working shifts in the parking garage.

While reading these books, a few lessons kept sprouting up everywhere:

- Relationships with other people are enormously important to succeeding at anything.

- The only way to stand out is to be different than those around you.

- You can change your circumstances by making a simple conscious decision to take the reins on your life.

With this new understanding of how to make things happen, I decided to just get started.

I had no clue what I was doing, but I was determined to make something happen for myself.

My first move was to reach out to everyone I knew who might be able to offer some advice.

Private teachers, professors, local freelancers, and anyone else I could think of.

Sure enough, people started giving me advice, and I began implementing it.

Fast forward to less than a year later, I was building relationships with lots of freelancers in the area, and I was teaching for organizations like the Philadelphia Orchestra.

With a little bit of luck and a lot of hard work, I was laying the foundation that would help me break into a whole new level of the freelancing world.

In what seemed like no time at all, I found myself playing gigs with groups that I thought were way out of my league when I first started.

It was in that period of my life I discovered that the solutions to the problems so many musicians face are incredibly simple, and I want to share those solutions with you.

My promise to you

My goal with this book is to give you the exact tactics I used to start and build a successful career as a freelancer.

There are plenty of books, blogs, experts, and classes out there preaching what is possible, but I want to show you how to get there.

By the time you finish this book, you will have everything you need to break into your local music scene.

All you have to do is make the choice to get started.

MYTHS OF FREELANCING

"The first principle is that you must not fool yourself and you are the easiest person to fool."

-Richard Feynman

Talent vs. Connections: where work really comes from

I vividly remember when I started noticing my classmates in school getting gigs and working around the area.

They were students (just like me), yet for some reason, they were getting called for gigs instead of me.

I couldn't help but wonder why.

We've all experienced gig envy at some point, and I'll be the first to admit that I had it bad.

Like, really bad.

So much so, that I'm embarrassed to even think about it.

Sitting in a practice room, I would often hear my friends in the hall talking about what gigs they were playing that weekend.

My mind would start buzzing with questions like:

Why didn't I get called for that gig?

Do they know someone that I don't?

Is it because they're older and more experienced?

Did I rub someone the wrong way?

At the time, I didn't know any better and had never experienced what it was like to be in the local scene as a freelancer.

Now, after years of struggling to figure out how to get work for myself, I discovered the secrets of where work actually comes from and how to get it.

Some time ago, I shared an article on Reddit about how to make contractors want to hire you.

A fellow musician commented that he would rather spend his time practicing and get hired because of his talent —rather than his social skills.

I understand where he was coming from, but he is missing the same thing I was missing in school.

If nobody knows you exist, then nobody will hire you.

How could they?

Getting hired as a musician is a combination of having the talent to play well *and* having connections with the people who will hire you.

Be careful not to fall into the trap of assuming if you just practice enough, you will get gigs.

While the ability to play well is absolutely necessary, the truth of the matter is, it is only one piece of the puzzle.

Without relationships with other musicians, contractors, and anyone else hiring musicians in your area, you won't get any work.

Many musicians might be tempted to fight the idea that connections help get work.

But just know, if you choose to believe that, you are only limiting yourself.

Now, please don't read this and think all you need to do is start passing out business cards.

It's not quite that simple, and I will share more about the most effective ways to build connections later.

At this point, as long as you are willing to acknowledge that talent and connections are both necessary, you are already well on your way to getting started as a freelancer.

Leave entitlement at the door

"A lot of people are so used to just seeing the outcome of work. They never see the side of the work you go through to produce the outcome."

-Michael Jackson

Before we dive too far into the strategies of this book, I have to get one thing out of the way.

It's uncomfortable, but for many people, it is necessary to say.

Just because you have a degree in music, have been playing guitar since high school, or studied with an awesome teacher, the world owes you nothing.

Frankly, things like degrees don't mean much at all.

What you bring to the table is what matters most.

People will hire you to do a job for them, and the only thing that matters is your ability to deliver.

Fancy degrees don't mean you deserve a gig over someone else.

At the end of the day, the musician who shows up on time, plays well, and is friendly to everyone, is the one who will likely get called back.

Speaking of school, don't complain that your school didn't prepare you for the real world.

That kind of thinking only breeds excuses that won't get you anywhere productive.

Whatever your situation might be, at the end of the day, it's *your* responsibility to take matters into your own hands and start creating the change you want for yourself.

BREAK INTO THE SCENE

Nobody is going to do it for you.

I can talk like this because I used to be that guy sitting around at parties complaining about these things.

If you're thinking *wow, what a loser,* you are absolutely right.

I had the mentality of a loser by blaming my problems on everyone but myself.

Things were tough for me in those days; however, once I made the conscious decision to take my future into my own hands, my life completely turned around.

A few months after I ditched that hindering sense of entitlement, I was instructing private students, playing my first few gigs, and creating opportunities that would later lead to launching my own business.

Everyone reading this knows somebody who's still stuck in that place of entitlement.

It might even be you.

That's all right because today is the day you can start reframing challenges and taking control of where your life is going.

FOCUS ON GETTING STARTED

"Action expresses priorities."

-Gandhi

You already have everything you need

One of the biggest mistakes musicians make when they try to get started freelancing is wasting an enormous amount of time and energy focusing on everything they don't have.

You've probably heard you must have a website, social media pages, and YouTube videos; but the truth is, you don't need any of that to get started.

This is a bit counterintuitive, I know.

All these things can be incredibly time consuming and won't generate immediate results.

This book is all about getting results as quickly as possible, so let's talk about where you should focus your time instead.

OK, so you're probably wondering what I mean by *you already have everything you need*.

Everyone has time, energy, a unique skill set, and most importantly—a natural network.

Time

People are extremely busy.

If you are in the position where you have even a little time on your hands, you can use that time to build your network and be valuable to others (more on this later).

Energy

Just like time, many working musicians are busy and lack the energy to do everything they'd like.

This is an opportunity for you to step in and be useful to someone else by taking something off their plate and doing it for them.

This is a great way to connect with others.

We will go further in depth later, but a few quick examples of this might be:

- Do librarian work for a local orchestra
- Be the stagehand for a recital
- Work the ticketing table at someone's gig

Unique perspective and skills

Along the same lines as time and energy, something else that everyone brings to the table is a unique perspective and skill set.

If someone you are interested in meeting is working on a project or has some issue they're trying to solve, no matter how small, an outside perspective could be just the thing they need.

We have all had the experience of getting so deep in the weeds of something that we develop tunnel vision.

Think about the skills and different perspective you have that might be of value to someone else.

Here are some examples to get your ideas flowing:

- Build a website for them
- Come up with a better way for them to sell CDs at their gigs
- Design a flyer or graphic they can use to promote events
- Research venues for them
- Set up a social media page for them
- Take photographs for them
- Write or edit for them

This list can go on and on, but these examples should get you thinking about ways you can add value to others using your unique perspective and skills.

Natural network

One of the most powerful tools you already have available to you is your natural network.

Now, when I say natural network, I am referring to people you naturally know through your day-to-day encounters.

It's easy to look at active freelancers and think *well, if I just knew those people, I could get work too.*

Does it help to know people?

Absolutely!

But when you're just beginning, you actually have plenty of relationships to help you get started.

More importantly, they're people who want to see you succeed.

Here are a few ideas of people you likely have in your natural network:

- Private instructors

- Professors from your school

- Classmates or colleagues

- Family members

- Friends

- Congregation members from church

- Coworkers at your job

- Anyone you met at previous gigs

You should make sure everyone in your natural network knows your goal to get started freelancing.

Most of these people will never directly pass a gig to you, but you never know when they might hear something and can pass your name along.

Don't assume that they will naturally think of you.

As much as we might like to think so, the people we know aren't always on the lookout for how they can help us out.

But if you just let your current connections know your goal, you will be amazed at the seemingly random opportunities that might come your way.

Making something out of nothing

While studying classical saxophone at the Boston Conservatory, a friend of mine named Karen Cubides discovered she was interested in learning about stage management.

There was only one glaring problem: she had very little experience as a stage manager.

Instead of waiting around for an opportunity that might never come around, Karen decided she was going to reach out to David Krauss from the MET Orchestra.

She volunteered to do all the stage manager work for the Berkshire Summer Music festival, which he runs.

Anyone familiar with stage management knows most people are

thrilled to have others do this work for them.

Since Karen was offering something of value, of course he agreed to let her come along.

When the festival came around, it turned out the majority of attendees were from Puerto Rico and were struggling to communicate in English.

Karen happens to speak Spanish and ended up translating throughout the week for many of the faculty members' lessons and masterclasses.

As you can imagine, she ended up being extremely valuable to everyone at the festival.

Due to her willingness to volunteer her time and energy as a stage manager, she was in a position to unexpectedly utilize her unique skill of Spanish, while building relationships with the faculty.

Currently, Karen runs her own artist management company called Cubides Artist Management, and many of the faculty members from that summer have been her clients.

As you can see, Karen was a perfect example of only using what she already had to create opportunities and work for herself.

Action Step:

Stop right now and take a moment to think about who you already have in your natural network.

We will dive much deeper into the topic of networking, but your goal here is to take the first step by recognizing the network you already have going for you.

Take a moment to write five people you already have in your network to work with.

1. _____

2. _____

3. _____

4. _____

5. _____

Things you can (and probably should) avoid

"I never worry about action, only inaction."

-Winston Churchill

When you get serious about building your freelance business, it's tempting to think you need to build a website, create social media pages, and order business cards.

Just about everyone you talk to will insist you must have all of these things as if they're the best way to market yourself.

I know many people will disagree with me, but I strongly encourage you to hold off on everything we are about to discuss.

Instead, you want to take all of your time, energy, and enthusiasm, and put it toward getting gigs as quickly as possible.

We have limited mental power to work with, so we want to make the most of it by focusing on strategies that will generate opportunities for you.

Setting up YouTube channels and picking website templates are only going to slow you down, stealing your precious mental energy.

All of these marketing strategies can be extremely valuable, but marketing comes later.

Additionally, to get the most value out of this book, I want you to embrace the mentality of *good enough* for this period of time when you're first getting started.

I know, many of you just cringed when you read good enough, but you'll see what I mean.

Musicians can spend hours perfecting a single position change or two measure passage, but you should approach this endeavor differently.

At this stage of the game, we are striving to establish credibility with the people who can hire us.

This can be done without the following items distracting your attention:

Websites

I'm going to let you in on a little secret.

Most people's websites, especially those of individual musicians, get very little traffic.

This means very few people actually visit the website, besides maybe the musician's mom and a few friends when they initially share it on Facebook.

Trust me, I have multiple websites and build websites for a wide variety of clients.

I've seen the analytics.

The number of people who will actually see your website in the beginning of your career launch is depressingly small.

It's counterintuitive, but I recommend that you skip a website altogether when you're just starting out.

You will quickly get overwhelmed when you realize you don't have a biography, pictures, recordings, repertoire lists, and everything else that can go on a website.

Eventually, you will have enough activity that a website will make sense.

But until then, don't let the website dominate your precious time.

Social media

How many times have you gotten an invitation on Facebook to like a friend's page?

Maybe you've even created a page yourself.

I have seen countless people build a page, invite all their friends to like it, then do one of two things:

First, after one week never update it again, thus, wasted a couple hours creating the page.

Second, this one is my personal favorite, constantly update the page and blast out event invitations to everyone they know, even people who live across the country.

There are endless options of social media platforms, and they will only continue to increase in number.

If you try to get yourself started on Facebook, Twitter, Snapchat, Instagram, YouTube, and SoundCloud, you will spend all your time setting up accounts and creating content, but never spend time doing things that actually drum up some work.

Just like a website, you will find social media sites are very time-consuming to create and maintain.

Headshots

While they might be great for a Facebook or online dating profile picture, professional photographs are completely unnecessary for individuals who are just getting started.

They do lend some professional credibility, but don't worry if you don't have them.

I know too many musicians with an abundance of glamour shots—but zero gigs.

Should you need a photograph, an iPhone picture will suffice.

Professional recordings

It has never been easier to make a superior quality recording with equipment you already own (even without much skill).

When I started out, my first goal was to pick up a few wedding gigs for a brass quintet with my friends.

At the time, I was convinced I needed to have recordings of the group before starting.

So, I made a few calls and managed to get a group together during my lunch break at work.

Armed with a measly Zoom recorder and a few junky arrangements of wedding tunes, we met for less than 20 minutes.

We read straight through everything, without even rehearsing.

That night I hacked together a sampler on my computer and sent it to a bunch of churches.

Within 24 hours we booked an Easter gig.

I easily could have overcomplicated this process and dragged it on for weeks, insisting on the perfect recording, but I decided to embrace the good enough mentality and just got it done.

All of these tools can be valuable, but when you're starting out, they're only going to slow you down from making real progress toward booking your first few gigs.

THE OPPORTUNITY MINDSET

"If opportunity doesn't knock, build a door."

-Milton Berle

How to identify and create opportunities

If there is one characteristic shared by all of the savviest musicians out there, it's their ability to look at the world around them and not only identify, but *create* their own opportunities.

People who know how to identify and create opportunities have an advantage over most of their peers.

They reap benefits for themselves while simultaneously creating opportunities for others.

This naturally builds their network.

By always looking for opportunities and adding value to their colleagues, a perpetual cycle is created of adding value to themselves and those around them.

We will discuss how to add value to others later, but having this advantageous mindset will change how you approach freelancing.

Once you make it a habit, you will quickly notice the positive effects it has on your career.

OK, so what exactly is an opportunity mindset?

An opportunity mindset is a way of thinking where you see everything around you as a potential opportunity.

This could be a chance to meet someone new, learn a new skill, or have a new experience.

There's not one specific way for everyone to practice this; it's unique for each individual.

The point is you always want to be on the lookout for opportunities to grow in some way.

One of the biggest challenges many people face when they start freelancing is operating under the assumption that gigs will just magically come to them because they can play their etudes and excerpts well.

This is absolutely, 100%, not the case.

In fact, it's not even close.

But here's the thing: almost every musician tends to think this way.

This, in itself, is a huge opportunity for you.

If you decide to consciously be on the lookout for chances to grow, you will quickly see the benefits appear in your life.

BREAK INTO THE SCENE

The reality is, you are either being proactive or reactive.

Only being reactive is the worst thing you can do when you are taking your first steps to launch a career.

Reactive means that you are reacting to things as they happen to you.

You're on defense—instead of offense.

When you're in this reactive, waiting around mode, you have no control over what is happening in your life.

Life is happening to you.

If you are just waiting around, the gigs you could be playing will get offered to other people.

Colleagues will be less likely to recommend you for things, and you'll have fewer opportunities in general.

Don't let this happen to you.

Take charge and be proactive instead.

When you are proactive, you go out and make things happen for yourself—instead of waiting around for things to happen to you.

People who get off the couch and go pound the pavement are the ones who win the freelance game.

In my first year out of school, I sent countless emails to anyone and everyone that I thought might be able to help me get started.

About 99% of those people never responded.

I bet most didn't even open the email, but that's not the point.

The point is that instead of waiting to get picked by someone else, I decided to go out there and create opportunities for myself.

And you know what?

It worked.

Within days of starting this proactive process, I was talking with people all over the area about Easter gigs, Christmas Eve gigs, and random special occasions people had coming up.

And let me tell you, after you get one gig, it's amazing how easily you can get another.

You'll start to meet other musicians at the gigs.

You'll meet people in the community, too.

And before you know it, you will have a network built from scratch.

It's a snowball effect that will continue throughout your career—if you make the decision to create your own opportunities.

And just think, once you start getting calls for work around town, you will be in the position to pass on work and recommend others, while also gaining tons of valuable experience.

It all starts with adopting an opportunity mindset.

BREAK INTO THE SCENE

Here's another example of always being on the lookout for opportunities from a friend of mine.

Early in my years as a freelancer, a good friend from school was working in a small grocery store on the outskirts of Philadelphia.

This was definitely not the type of job you would expect to lead to freelance work.

But as luck would have it, that little town has a Dickens themed Christmas festival every year.

And for that festival, they hire a brass ensemble to perform.

The manager of this grocery store was in charge of hiring vendors for the event.

Since my friend happened to have a relationship with the person hiring, we got the gig.

I know what you're thinking, *does that mean a rag tag bunch of costumed brass players?*

Yes, that's exactly what it means.

Ridiculous hats aside, there is a great lesson to be learned here.

A grocery store seems like the last place a freelance opportunity would come from; nonetheless, it led to a yearly gig that actually pays very well.

One year there was a major blizzard during the festival.

Even though many people were going home, we stuck around and played in the midst of blizzard.

This blew the festival attendees away, and they have since hired us many times.

Keep in mind that this is the type of gig where you interact with large numbers of people.

One year I met a man who expressed interest in having our group perform at his office Christmas party.

I didn't have a business card on me, so I took his name and email address.

Within minutes, I followed up by emailing him from my phone.

We were discussing the specifics of the event by the end of the day.

This man turned out to be the dean of one of the largest medical schools in Philadelphia, and our group was hired to play at a Christmas party for one of their many hospitals in the region.

By being proactive, I secured another gig and began building a relationship with a very influential individual in the area.

You just never know who you are going to meet or what opportunities those encounters will lead to.

Was this a random encounter?

Yes and no.

It was random in the sense that this individual happened to be there.

However, when you keep an open mind and are proactive, good things will happen to you.

How to get lucky

"I've always understood luck to be where opportunity meets preparation."

-Casey Neistat

I used to think that a former roommate of mine was the luckiest guy alive.

Several early Sunday mornings each month, I heard him leave the house, and I had no idea where he was going.

Then one day I learned all those early morning trips were to play church services in the area.

When he revealed this, I was totally blown away.

How did he get all of these gigs?

He explained that he reached out to about 100 different churches to let them know he was available to play if they ever needed music for a service.

That probably took him a few hours one afternoon, and he was getting paying gigs from that afternoon's work for months.

I learned an incredible lesson that day.

Luck has very little to do with chance.

This guy wasn't lucky at all.

He was simply creating his own opportunities.

The luckiest people are those who put themselves in the position to get opportunities.

Everybody knows someone who appears incredibly lucky, but the reality is, the majority of those with lots of opportunities have either been working harder or longer than you.

Your actions over time will dramatically impact how lucky you are in the future.

Most musicians tend to falsely believe if they just practice their scales or concertos, the professional work will magically come their way.

It doesn't matter what school you went to or which teacher you studied with.

Your musical talent is only one piece of the puzzle, and you need the other pieces too.

The good news is anyone can put themselves in the position to get lucky—if they choose to do so.

The sooner you start meeting people and developing the skills laid out in this book, the sooner you will be able to take advantage of opportunities when they come your way.

WHAT TYPES OF WORK
ARE THERE?

The day I announced I was going into a music career was the day everyone (who had been telling me for 10 years how amazing it was that I was so into music) began questioning my decision.

What used to be praise and support quickly shifted to nervous energy and doubts about what I wanted to study at college.

Suddenly, questions that never seemed relevant before became common conversational topics.

Are you sure you want to make music a career?

Isn't that more of a hobby?

What will you do to pay the bills?

How much money do musicians even make?

Do you have a backup plan?

The list of questions laced with doubt went on and on, and to be honest, I didn't have a good answer for any of them.

In fact, it took me several years to truly understand what the options were for musicians.

It took even longer to learn how to get my foot in the door and land work.

Whether you are a principal player in a major symphony orchestra, touring the world with your band, a music teacher who freelances on the side, or a student starting from scratch, I think we can all agree that, at some point, we were clueless about our options in music.

There is a wide variety of options for work as a musician.

So many, that I couldn't possibly think of them all.

But this section is meant to get you thinking about options that might appeal to you.

Since everyone's interests and situations are unique, I will lay out a bunch of ideas to hopefully help you understand the various ways professional musicians—just like you—are making money every day.

These lists are not intended to be comprehensive.

The goal is to simply get you thinking about what's possible.

Once you gain awareness of the opportunities around you, you will start noticing the type of gigs other people are doing.

Take a look at websites, schedules, and events to see what people are up to, not only locally, but all over the world.

The people who are constantly looking for new and different kinds of work are almost always the busiest freelancers.

BREAK INTO THE SCENE

Performing

Outside of the obvious example of winning an audition, there are tons of different performance opportunities out there:

- Church concert series
- Church services
- Commencement ceremonies
- Community choirs
- Community theater productions
- Conservatories, colleges, and universities (bands, orchestras, choirs) as a substitute
- Cruise ship groups
- High school musical productions
- Holiday caroling groups
- Holiday parties
- Private parties
- Regional orchestras
- Retirement communities
- Weddings (bands, cocktail hours, ceremonies)
- Wind ensembles
- Youth orchestras as a substitute

37

Teaching

- Audition prep coach
- Create an online course
- Educational performances (create one or work for existing programs through local orchestras)
- El Sistema-inspired programs
- Group lessons
- Lead sectionals (local schools, youth orchestras, colleges, and universities)
- Local music schools
- Music theory classes
- Private lessons
- Skype lessons
- Teaching artist work for local nonprofits
- Work with marching bands

Miscellaneous

- Audio engineer
- Build and manage websites
- Compose your own arrangements
- Contract orchestras
- Input parts into Finale or Sibelius

- Librarian work
- Repair instruments
- Stagehand service
- Transcribe scores
- Transpose parts for different ensembles
- Tune pianos
- Write grants

Does it matter where you live?

Yes and no.

The question of location is a common one because different places offer different opportunities.

Geography can make a big difference, so you should take time to consider how location factors into your career aspirations.

Everyone has different goals in their musical life.

Some people want a backyard and to teach lessons from their home.

Others want to play as much as they possibly can and don't mind sharing a small apartment with four roommates.

It's all about what *you* value.

Anybody with a computer or smartphone can teach video lessons, but the same doesn't go for subbing on Broadway.

If you want to play on Broadway, move to New York City.

Or if you want to get into the film music scene, you might move to a city where studios record live orchestras.

Do those opportunities excite you?

If so, great.

However, if you know that the opportunities you want to pursue are not available in your current location, then perhaps a move is in your future.

It's your life.

Take control of it and do what's best for you.

As for me, I grew up in South Carolina where there is very little classical music.

When I went away to college my entire world changed.

I experienced life in a city with an amazing orchestra and a wealth of other things to immerse myself in.

For me, moving to Philadelphia for college was one of the best decisions I ever made.

It might be totally different for you.

To some, the idea of driving two hours to a gig is enough to just not bother playing, while others don't mind it at all.

There's no right or wrong answer with location.

You must identify what's important to you and go with a location and opportunities that make the most sense for you.

BREAKING MENTAL BARRIERS

"You start out as a phony and become real."

-Glenn O'Brien

Here lies the most challenging concept in this book.

I am willing to bet there are things in your life you know you *should* be doing, but for whatever reason, you aren't.

Whether you are facing irrational fears, procrastination, or straight up excuses, the greatest challenge when doing something out of your comfort zone is getting past your own mental barriers.

The stories we tell ourselves are always worse than the actual outcomes.

It's easy to stay in our comfort zone.

That's why most people do it.

The reality is that most people never bother trying to make progress with things like freelancing.

I get it.

It can be scary at first.

And when you sit down to send out your first email, it will be tough.

Sometimes you will get rejected—and that's OK.

Once you take that first leap, though, I guarantee you will see that it isn't so bad.

The worst case scenarios never turn into reality.

Opportunities don't just magically appear; you have to put yourself out there and create them.

Getting past our own mental barriers is the first step to making progress, and once you get that first bit of momentum, you will quickly find that it's not nearly as bad as you feared.

Trust me, I know.

I have been there—paralyzed by the stories I was telling myself.

The next section is dedicated to addressing the stories we tell ourselves to avoid taking action.

Common mental barriers and how to conquer them

"We're all terrified of being revealed as amateurs."

-Austin Kleon

"I'm not ready"

You never will be, so don't even worry about this one.

It doesn't matter if you don't have a ton of experience, or if you are an enthusiast who only wants to pick up a few weekend gigs.

You will fail many times when you are getting started, so it's best to just get those out of the way as soon as possible.

Nobody is ever really ready for something new.

Sometimes you just have to make the choice that you are going to do it—and figure out the rest as you go.

"I'm not good enough"

Yes, you are.

You might not feel like it, but you are.

You don't have to be the best to get started.

Are you ready to play guest principal with the Boston Symphony?

Maybe, but maybe not.

And you know what?

That's totally fine.

This book is meant to help you take the first steps, and one of those is to understand what types of freelance work are available to you.

Everybody starts somewhere, and throughout this book, you will learn how to identify the opportunities around you.

There are gigs out there for all different levels of talent; and even if you are a high school student, there is work out there that you can do to get started.

You don't need a fancy degree from a conservatory to play weddings, church services, or community theater productions.

As you understand the options available to you, you will quickly start to spot opportunities out there for musicians at any level.

They may not all be glamorous, but they will give you a place to start—and that is what's important.

"It's not the right time"

The right time doesn't exist.

There, I said it.

Everyone has different responsibilities in their life.

You might be reading this as a freshman at a state school.

Or maybe you have a family, student loans, and a mortgage payment each month.

I won't pretend to understand or have the answers to everyone's situation.

One thing I know is if you wait around for the perfect time, you will never do anything but wait around.

There will always be a million reasons why you can't or shouldn't do something.

Frankly, the longer you wait to do something, the less likely it is that you will do it.

Don't wait around for the right time because it isn't coming.

Someday never comes.

Let go of the doubt and just get started today.

"I don't want to take other people's work"

If you are just starting out as a freelancer, this should be the least of your concerns.

It takes time to establish credibility in any community of freelancers.

In all honesty, you probably won't get called for the best gigs in town at first, so don't let that worry you.

Be real with yourself about the likelihood of taking work away from others.

The best freelancers already have relationships with the people and places they work in town, and it's unlikely that you will take their gigs.

With that being said, please don't be the person who actively pursues other people's work.

That's a guaranteed way to build bad rapport in your scene.

There are a few weekends every year it seems everyone is going to be working.

A great goal when starting out is to get yourself working on those weekends when there never seems to be enough players.

In the world of Christmas Eve and Easter gigs, anyone with a brass instrument in their closet and a pulse could get hired to play a church service.

You should just focus on getting yourself out there among your future colleagues and connecting with them in an authentic way.

The work will come if you follow the steps outlined in this book.

Fear of rejection

I spent years of my life talking about what I was *going* to do, but never actually *doing* anything.

The problem wasn't a lack of ideas or knowledge of what I needed to do.

If I'm being totally honest, I was afraid of rejection.

When you put yourself out there and try something new, it is terrifying because it immediately opens you up to the possibility of rejection.

That fear crippled me for years.

These debilitating thoughts seemed to constantly repeat in my head:

What if other people find out that I failed?

How do I know this is even worth a try?

What if I rub someone the wrong way and never get hired?

Doing nothing may feel safe and comfortable, but it will not get you anywhere.

Conquer these mental barriers

The key to getting past all of these barriers is to start small.

Don't worry about reaching out to everyone; focus on reaching out to one person.

After you have reached out to one person, you can bump it up to five.

Once you get comfortable with putting yourself out there, you will find that nothing bad will happen to you.

Even though it took me a while to get going, when I finally did, it completely changed the course of my life as a musician.

My first project was essentially trying to pick up brass quintet gigs.

What kind of gigs?

Honestly, I had no idea.

It didn't matter because I just wanted to be working.

If you have ever gotten to the point where you were fed up with something and couldn't take it anymore, then you know how I felt on the day I decided to finally take matters into my own hands.

After years of frustration and expecting something to happen, I decided that I was finally ready to push aside all the fear and just get started.

I spent hours researching and finding the contact information for hundreds of churches, wedding planners, and concert series.

What started as one of the scariest things I had ever done quickly turned into one of the most exciting things I had experienced in my career at the time.

Of those hundreds of emails, I would say more than 90% of them never responded, and only one or two people asked me not to reach out again.

But guess what happened.

I started getting offers for gigs.

After years of talking about what I was *going* to do and wishing that people would call me, I decided to get out there and just do it myself.

Don't get me wrong.

This was not easy.

Well, in a sense, it was incredibly easy to do.

The physical act of executing the idea wasn't the challenging part.

Getting past all of the horror stories I was telling myself was the real obstacle.

I've found consequences are always worse in your head than they are in reality.

Sadly, most people will never see the reality of their ideas because they'll never take action.

Until you actually get turned down from something, don't waste your time worrying about rejection.

If you get far enough along where people are telling you "no," then you should pat yourself on the back because that means you're putting in the effort to get going—and that is a huge achievement.

When I sent out all those emails, I fully expected some kind of backlash.

In reality, the majority were completely ignored and nothing happened.

But guess what.

Even though most were ignored, I ended up getting several offers for Christmas and Easter services that year.

By just pushing past the mental barriers and getting started, I got myself, and several friends, booked for a couple of gigs.

As soon as you can accept that rejection is just part of the process, and it's not nearly as scary as you think, you will be well on your way to getting yourself started.

When rejection does occur, take it as an opportunity to grow by trying to understand why it didn't work.

If you have the opportunity to, ask if they have any feedback that you can use the next time around.

It could be something as simple as asking at the wrong time or asking the wrong person.

Use that feedback to continuously improve what you are doing and move on to the next opportunity.

You never know what you might learn by just asking for feedback.

Don't play the comparison game

Do you ever scroll through your social media feeds, see pictures of people you went to school with at awesome gigs, and get secretly jealous?

Yeah, me too.

One of the most challenging things when you're trying to get started in a career like music is to not get discouraged by the successes you see around you.

I've been there, and it still happens to me more than I'd like.

It's really hard to resist comparing yourself to others.

Yet, playing the comparison game is a total waste of your time and mental energy.

BREAK INTO THE SCENE

You will always lose the comparison game—so don't even bother.

There will always be someone getting a cooler opportunity or making more money than you.

Instead of harboring resentment, maybe you could ask them for advice instead.

Learning from someone who does what you want to do is far more productive than being jealous of them.

We all have our struggles.

We just don't post about them on the Internet.

Now, to be clear, I have no qualms about what you or anyone else decides to post on social media.

It's your space, and you can do whatever you want with it.

The point is that comparing yourself to what other people are doing is counterproductive and will only slow you down.

Everyone has their own path to take, and it doesn't matter how it compares to the snapshot people share of their lives online.

Do your own thing and work at your own pace.

Try to be better today than you were yesterday.

That might mean making one more connection, booking one more gig, gaining one more student, or asking advice from someone you admire.

Celebrate all of the progress you make and focus on continuing to improve.

We have different journeys and destinations, so make the most out of yours and don't worry about what other people are doing.

With a little hard work and persistence, you might be the person others look to for inspiration.

TIME MANAGEMENT AND GOALS

*"It's not that we have a short time to live, but that
we waste a lot of it."*

-Seneca

Designating time vs. Finding time

I don't have time.

This is one of the most common lies that we tell ourselves and others.

That's right, it's a lie.

And today is the day to start telling the truth.

While I don't think anyone means to lie about their time, almost everyone does.

We use this excuse to justify why we don't do things.

Maybe you haven't started looking for a new job yet, called your mom once a week, or done something as simple as going to the grocery store.

Whatever the case may be, specifics aren't important.

What is important is that we start being real with ourselves about what we value enough to designate time for it in our schedules.

If you truly want to achieve something, you must designate time to focus on it.

We have all said, "Oh, I need to find the time to do ..." at some point.

Your goal should not be to *find* the time.

Your goal should be to *designate* time so that whatever you need to do actually gets done.

When someone says they don't have time for something, what they really mean is they don't want to make time to do it.

The President of the United States has the same number of hours each day as everyone else; the only difference is how individuals choose to use time.

Think about this for a moment: How much time each day do you spend watching TV, playing video games, or mindlessly scrolling through social media feeds?

Probably a lot.

This isn't to say that you should never do these things.

The point is, if you are serious about building a career as a freelancer, it's going to take an investment of time.

Being honest with yourself about your priorities and making sure you invest the necessary time are the first strides to taking action.

BREAK INTO THE SCENE

The simplest way to get started is to identify a time in your schedule and block it off to focus on the strategies and action steps in this book.

It could be during a commute, on your lunch break, or a Sunday evening.

Choose a time.

Commit to it.

And follow through.

You can use the calendar app on your phone to designate the time and set yourself a reminder.

Whenever you are working, turn your phone off, close your social media tabs on your browser (I know they're there), and focus.

Just think, if you send five emails to potential contacts each week, by the end of one year, you will have reached out to 260 new people.

Even if only a handful of people respond and connect with you, that's still a huge win.

It doesn't matter when you do it, or how you do it; the only thing that matters is that you get it done.

When I finally sat down to research and send out that first batch of emails, I held myself accountable by asking my friends to get together to record a sampler.

This accomplished two things:

First, it held me accountable because my friends invested time into helping me, so I didn't want to let them down.

Second, I forced a timeline on myself by telling them I would start trying to get us hired as soon as I had the recording.

Committing yourself to something is powerful when trying to hold yourself accountable.

There are countless books and psychological studies on the topic of commitment, but all you really need to know is when you commit yourself to something, you are considerably more likely to follow through.

If you aren't sure how to hold yourself accountable, simply start by designating time in your calendar to start implementing the material you learn in this book.

Action Step

Open your calendar and look at your schedule.

Find a block of time to designate as your time to focus on getting started as a freelancer.

Even this small action step will help you start making progress by deciding on a time that you will commit to doing the work covered in this book.

Go for the small wins first

*"The man who moves a mountain begins by carrying
away small stones."*

-Confucius

Let's talk about goals.

This isn't the typical shoot for the moon and you'll land among the stars kind of goal setting.

I want to set you up for success by setting simple goals that can help get you started freelancing as soon as possible.

Don't overwhelm yourself by trying to do too much at once.

Instead, set yourself up for success by allowing yourself to get your first small wins.

A small win could be something as simple as getting a $100 gig or one student to sign up for weekly lessons.

Of course, you will shoot for larger goals later on, but nobody starts out as a busy freelancer.

It's a series of small wins that build the foundation careers are built upon.

When I was just getting started as a freelancer, I spent too much time trying to do too many things at once.

I was trying to get in touch with contractors, start my own quintet, build a private studio, and become a teaching artist all at the same time.

As a result of spreading myself too thin, I got nowhere on any of these endeavors.

I finally made some progress when I started focusing on simpler, more specific objectives.

The first step for me was trying to get a brass quintet off the ground by reaching out to anyone who might need a quintet (as I previously covered).

Next, I put everything else aside and asked my private teacher if he could introduce me to people who might share advice on how to get started teaching in the area.

By focusing on one thing at a time, I was able to direct all of my attention on one task and successfully connect with people who could offer me guidance about what to do next.

Within just a few months of my outreach to people about my brass quintet and teaching work, I made connections that would ultimately lead to my first gigs in both areas.

When thinking about your own goals, get incredibly specific with what you are trying to achieve as a freelancer because once you know where you're going, you can start to create the roadmap to get there.

Too many people say things like, "I just want to do any kind of gig."

Without a clear goal, you'll be mindlessly stumbling around as you dabble in a little bit of everything and make minimal progress.

Once you are clear where you are headed, and you secure one gig, you can more easily get another.

If you can get 2, then you can get 10, or 50, or 100 over time.

Getting those first wins will not only give you a sense of direction, but they will also validate that the work you are doing is indeed leading you where you want to go.

So here's the question: What is the first small goal you want to achieve?

Landing a wedding gig?

Picking up a private student?

Working for a marching band?

Subbing with a local orchestra?

Get specific about where you are going, and let's start drawing the map to get you there.

Action Step

In the spirit of goal setting, take a moment right now and decide where you're going to focus your energy to get your first small win.

Whatever type of work you plan to invest in, view the rest of the book from that perspective.

You can always change it up as you go, but for now, let's be as specific as possible.

Write your first small goal below:

_____

_____

_____

_____

MAKING CONNECTIONS

"Call it a clan, call it a network, call it a tribe, call it family. Whatever you call it, whoever you are, you need one."

-Jane Howard

Build it before you need it

A common misconception about networking is that you should only meet people and actively pursue new connections when you need them.

This is totally backwards.

By avoiding this mistake and getting started today, you will lay the foundation for successful networking before most people even start to think about it.

It doesn't matter if you are currently in school, about to move to a new city, or are already freelancing; the time to start cultivating relationships is right now.

Your network will be a source of countless opportunities throughout your career, so the sooner you get started, the better off you will be.

This portion of the book is where you are going to start authentically building these connections or expanding the network you already have.

You will need to know folks in the local scene, so let's go ahead and get your game plan together.

Remember, opportunities are a combination of knowing the right people and having the skill set to do the job well.

Waiting until you need something is not a great time to reach out to someone.

You run the risk of coming off as desperate, and they will sense that you're only contacting them because you want something from them.

It's ideal if you can come from an angle of bringing value to those around you.

Give way more than you take.

The people who do this are few and far between.

I promise that if you are consistently useful to those around you, people will want you around.

What's important is actively creating genuine relationships with others.

When you are just getting started, you have yet to prove yourself to the players in your area.

It takes time to establish credibility among your future colleagues, so there is no better time than right now to get started.

Social skills matter

The idea that people get calls for gigs exclusively for their talent is a nice thought but has no basis in reality.

If you fight this truth, you are only making it more difficult for yourself to succeed in the world of freelancing because your ability to connect with your colleagues has a direct impact on the amount of work you get.

Poor social skills can be the deciding factor in whether or not you are called back.

That sounds harsh, but it's the truth.

It doesn't matter if you are shy or outgoing; social skills can easily be learned and improved.

Some people are naturally good with others, while the rest of us may have to try a little harder.

You don't have to have amazing social skills.

They just have to be good enough to make positive impressions on those around you.

I have met many people in my life as a freelancer that have an awful time getting called back to gigs because of their complete lack of social awareness.

Like it or not, people are constantly making judgments on others based on everything from how they dress, how well they play, or even how clean their car is.

I'm not saying it's right or wrong; it just is.

Instead of fighting it, accept it and use it to your advantage.

When interacting with new colleagues, doing a few simple things could be the difference between leaving a great impression or them avoiding eye contact with you in the bathroom at intermission.

The first time you meet people, they have no preconceived notion of who you are.

However, the moment they see how you interact with your environment, they will begin to form opinions.

This is an opportunity and your responsibility to help craft the image you want people to see.

Simply smiling at people across the room is enough to start forming a positive impression.

I like to think about social behavior at gigs on a spectrum.

On one end you have the people who are extremely shy and keep to themselves.

The other end of the spectrum is the overly aggressive schmoozers trying to force relationships out of thin air.

My advice is shoot for somewhere in the middle.

BREAK INTO THE SCENE

If you're reading this and cringing at the thought of having to be something you're not, don't worry.

There are a few simple things that anyone can do to improve their social skills while still being authentic.

Introduce yourself first

You don't have to wait for others to come to you.

When you make the first move to greet and introduce yourself, it sends a positive vibe and you appear more confident.

Many people have anxiety about making introductions, so they just might view it as a favor if you take the burden from them by saying a friendly hello first.

Make eye contact

This is different than staring.

Please don't stare.

Something as simple as making eye contact while speaking with people or passing them in the hall can make a positive difference.

And eye contact is something anyone can do.

You know that moment you felt an instant connection when you happened to meet someone's gaze from across the room?

It is amazing how much simple eye contact can improve the dynamic of an interaction.

Shake hands

Don't be shy about reaching out to shake someone's hand.

An appropriately firm grip makes a better impression than just saying hello.

Having said that, we've all shaken hands with someone who has a death grip.

Don't make people wince after you greet them.

Yet, don't give someone a limp handshake where they feel like they're squeezing a dead fish either.

They'll remember a death grip or a limp fish grip, but not for a good reason.

Instead, go for a grip somewhere in-between.

This might seem like a tiny detail, but I promise it will make a difference.

Smile

If there's one thing that can dramatically improve other people's perception of you, it's smiling.

Even someone sitting across the room, without exchanging a word, can form a positive impression of you if the person sees you smiling.

I always thought this was odd, but a lot of people rarely smile.

It doesn't matter if your personality tends to be more introverted or extroverted.

A smile sends the signal that you are happy to be there, and it gives off a friendly vibe.

Try smiling at everyone you walk by on the street today.

I bet you will notice a difference in their expression after you smile at them.

Use people's names

The sweetest sound in the world to everyone is their name.

Maybe it secretly tickles their ego.

I have no idea.

But one thing I know is that people love to be called by their name.

The next time you introduce yourself to someone, make a mental note to remember their name.

When you see them later on your way out, use their name as you say goodbye.

Very few people bother to remember names anymore.

I make lists of people's names in my phone to help me remember those around me.

Sometimes I even make notes about what we talked about.

That might sound silly, but people will be blown away when you run into them a year later and remember their name and what you talked about.

The substitute that I will never call again

I once had a situation beyond my control that required me to drop everything and find substitutes for a busy weekend of work.

Because it was a such a busy weekend, all of my usual substitutes were unavailable.

A few months prior to this, a guy who was new in town contacted me about subbing if I ever needed a player.

This person was a tremendous help to me since he filled in at various rehearsals and concerts, so I was thrilled to pass him the work.

It all seemed great.

Well, after the hectic weekend was over, I ran into some of the folks from that weekend's gigs.

To my dismay, they had negative things to say about him.

And these weren't just petty things.

People commented on how rude he was to members of the section and even to the staff of the ensembles.

Situations like this can reflect poorly on the person who made the recommendation (in this case, me).

How you interact with your colleagues is important because so much of your credibility in the freelance world comes from other people's perceptions of you.

Contractors ask the players and other contractors they trust for recommendations.

If the people they ask don't like working with you, then your invitations to play could be minimal.

This particular substitute will never get a call from me again.

He will probably not be recommended by any of the players he was rude to either.

Little things while interacting with others make all the difference.

Whether it's simply introducing yourself with a smile or making a mental note to remember a name, always do your best to leave a good impression on those you meet.

It's not about knowing everyone

"The trick is not caring about what everyone thinks of you and just caring about what the right people think of you."

-Brian Michael Bendis

Many people operate under the false assumption that in order to have a great network of colleagues, they have to know everyone.

Sure, it helps to have a large circle of connections, but it is unnecessary when you're early in your career and trying to get started.

Even professionals who have been playing for many years will tell you most of their work comes from only a few places.

One solid connection with someone who likes you and genuinely wants to see you succeed is all you need to get going.

Charlie Hoehn, a friend and mentor of mine, said it best on his blog with just a few simple sentences:

> "The best networkers don't call it *networking*. They don't *build relationships*.
>
> They call it *being friends*. And they *help people*."

This has been true for me and the majority of the well-connected people I know.

Actively trying to network with people almost always comes across as fake—and people know it.

When you connect with those around you in a meaningful way, you develop genuine relationships.

Building a great network takes time, but it should always start from a place of creating authentic relationships with people.

Just one person inviting you to a gig is enough to get you started.

Networks compound over time, so don't worry if you don't know a ton of people yet.

When I say networks compound, I mean each gig you play will be a chance to meet new people and make new friends, which will often lead to new opportunities.

Every time you show up to a gig, be friendly to everyone.

Be the person people want to work with, and you will be amazed how fast your circle of acquaintances—and access to opportunities—grows.

The secret to building an amazing network

"There's only one rule I know of ... you've got to be kind."

-Kurt Vonnegut

Those who have amazing opportunities will likely tell you every cool thing they've done somehow came from someone else.

We have all heard it before.

"It's all about who you know."

But here's the thing: that saying is wrong.

It's not really about who you know.

It's actually about who you have *relationships* with.

That might sound like I'm being picky, but there is a huge difference.

We all know tons of people.

But just because someone knows you, does not mean they're going to recommend you for a gig or send students your way.

I'm going to share a secret with you.

Building an amazing network is all about adding value to those around you.

That's it.

Don't be that person at events who is schmoozing nonstop and pushing their business cards all over the room.

We probably all know people like this.

Engaging with others in a self-serving way will often have the opposite effect than intended.

The people with the largest networks are people who bring the most value to those around them, giving much more than they get in return.

Too many people approach networking as a transactional process.

If you are going into meeting someone with an expectation of getting something out of them, it will almost never pan out the way you want.

Instead, approach people by being friendly and looking for ways to add value to them, and just watch how much quicker you are able to connect.

So, you are probably wondering what I mean by adding value.

It's not a simple answer because it means something different to everyone you meet.

Basically, try to identify what people care about, and by just making an effort, you will be in a better position.

How to add value, even if you're new

Pass work to others

This is the fastest way to connect with essentially any working musician.

I have never met a musician who wouldn't appreciate someone sending work their way.

No matter what level they are on, just about everyone could use a little extra work.

If you can be that source of work, you will rapidly build your network.

As humans, we are wired for reciprocation.

When someone gives us something, we naturally want to return the favor.

The power of reciprocation is a well-known and powerful psychological phenomenon.

Regardless of how well you know people, if you pass work to them, you have a great chance they will return the favor.

Always recommend others

There are few things more disappointing than having to turn down a gig.

While this can be a major bummer, it's actually a great opportunity to bring value to others.

Whenever a contractor reaches out to you and you can't take the gig, always respond with a list of recommendations of other people they can ask.

This is not only enormously valuable for the contractor, but it doubles as a chance for you to pass work to someone else.

Now you've doubled your reciprocation and added value to multiple people at once.

If you have ever been responsible for hiring, then you know what a pain it can be when you are running out of people to call because nobody is available.

Let's pretend you play the violin, and the contractor is a trombonist.

Chances are you know more violinists than the contractor.

After thanking the contractor for thinking of you, send a list of recommendations of others that simply reads:

Name: musician@email.com

Name: musician@email.com

Name: musician@email.com

Name: musician@email.com

Name: musician@email.com

VISIT BREAKINTOTHESCENE.COM/BONUSES *FOR AN EXACT EMAIL SCRIPT THAT YOU CAN EASILY COPY AND PASTE FROM.*

The more names you give, the more likely the contractor can find someone, which is a win for everyone involved.

Contractors will love you for doing this.

Moreover, even though you couldn't take that gig, you could get called again just because you were helpful.

It's a simple extra step that could rapidly build your network of both contractors and colleagues around town, perhaps even those you haven't met yet.

Pass work to those who can return the favor

This is one of the best pieces of advice I have received.

As you start passing work off to your soon-to-be colleagues, you will quickly learn who plays the various gigs around town.

This brings us to a very important point that most people will miss.

Whenever you recommend others, recommend those who are active in your scene.

Because of the natural desire to reciprocate, you have a better chance of the favor being returned in the future.

For example, if there is a local orchestra you would love to sub with, recommend everybody who plays in that group whenever you can.

Those who are working a lot in town are important people to know and recommend because when they turn down gigs, they just might pass them to you.

Eventually, you will meet these people and have the opportunity to start building rapport.

Maybe they will eventually hire you; maybe they won't.

It's not going to work out every time, and that's OK.

Keep in mind, if you are a young freelancer, you won't likely get called to play for the top gigs in your area.

That's all right because even people who play the bigger gigs are probably doing some work in the area that you could get called for.

When I first started out, I recommended every person I could for gigs that I had to turn down.

Some of those contacts quickly became people I got to know, while others took a few years.

It only takes a couple minutes to go above and beyond everyone else, yet it has a substantial impact.

My constant stream of recommendations has led to great relationships with many people in my local area, both personally and professionally.

Attend their gigs

When I was graduating from school, I realized that I knew very few people in the area outside of my friends from school.

Whether you are a recent graduate, new to a city, or just want to expand your network, attending gigs of other people is a fantastic way to meet them.

It doesn't matter if it's a masterclass, a jazz club, or a recital at a local church; everyone welcomes a larger audience.

My first big push, which actually launched me into my first several teaching jobs, was attending local community engagement activities.

In an effort to learn what opportunities were out there, I reached out to the individuals involved in these organizations and asked if I could attend and observe their classes or performances.

At the time, I didn't realize how unusual this was.

Just by showing up consistently, with no expectation other than to learn, I got my foot in the door of community engagement and was exposed to the wonderful world of teaching artistry.

On top of that, I stumbled into an entire section of the classical music industry that I didn't even know existed.

The beauty of this is it only requires a fraction of your time, and you can easily combine this strategy with others outlined in the book.

It also allows you to meet people in a context that is more conducive to building relationships.

If someone you want to meet is playing a few recitals, just go observe.

Say hello, congratulate the performers after the performance, and follow up with them afterward about how awesome it was to meet them.

Which brings us to our final strategy for adding value, even if you're new: follow up.

Always follow up

Following up with people is another thing I've learned is unbelievably rare, especially when people don't have a ton to offer others yet.

Passing out business cards is ineffective because you want to be the person to follow up with them, not the other way around.

In all my years working as a freelancer, I honestly can't think of a single time that I handed someone a business card and was hired for a gig because of it.

On the other hand, I can think of many times I obtained work because I was the only person to follow up.

Like almost everything we have discussed in this book, this tactic will work simply because it is uncommon.

Be the person that always follows up.

A lesson from an 11th grader

One time I was guest speaking about entrepreneurship for a local youth orchestra where the audience was comprised of local high school students.

I spoke about the same strategies discussed in this book.

As I often do, I challenged these students to simply email me and follow up after the presentation.

I have given this talk many times.

The audience has ranged from young music students to graduate students, and only *one* person has ever followed up with me.

This sounds crazy, I know.

But the only person to ever send me that follow up email was an 11th grade trumpet player from Philadelphia.

You might think I am exaggerating—but I'm not.

A 16-year-old student is the only person who followed through.

Plenty of people have nodded their heads and said they were going to reach out, but he's the only one who actually took action.

The lesson here is by doing something as simple as following up with people, you can stand out from the crowd.

It is that uncommon.

It doesn't have to be complicated or difficult to get someone's attention.

Sometimes, it just takes being the person to follow through.

Go where the fish are

"Spectacular achievement is always preceded by spectacular preparation."

-Robert H. Schuller

Some of the best advice I have ever heard about building your network has nothing to do with networking, yet, in a way, has everything to do with it.

BREAK INTO THE SCENE

If you want to catch a fish, then go where the fish are.

This is fantastic advice if you aren't sure who you should be connecting with.

While it is a seemingly obvious concept, it's one that gets overlooked by most people (including myself, once upon a time).

When I first started out, I noticed there was a small circle of people who had just about every kind of gig locked in.

I knew there were a ton of working musicians in town I needed to get to know.

But I didn't know who they were, and I definitely didn't know how to get in touch with them.

Then one day I heard this piece of advice about going where the fish are.

After spending months spinning my wheels, getting nowhere, I finally realized that the majority of the work I was doing came from local colleges and universities that needed musicians to fill their ensembles for performance.

This might not sound like a big deal, but it was a major breakthrough in my freelancing career.

That day I reached out to every single college in the region with a simple email letting them know if they ever needed an additional horn player, I was available and would love to play.

I heard back from almost every college's music department within the next few weeks.

They didn't all hire me.

But over the next few months, I began getting emails about gigs I didn't even know existed before.

This strategy was introduced to me through the work of blogger and author Ramit Sethi.

Without further ado, let's get started.

The fishing hole strategy

This strategy is all about finding the hubs of information where you can quickly learn the landscape of the space you are interested in.

When you are doing this research, the most important factor in finding a successful fishing hole is to know exactly what you are looking for.

For the sake of clarity, I'll share a few brief examples.

Individual musicians looking for work should be looking for established ensembles in their area, which can include anything from choral groups and orchestras to wedding bands.

If you are looking for opportunities for a group, I recommend looking for places with event planners, venues that feature similar groups, or existing concert series.

BREAK INTO THE SCENE

Music teachers looking for more opportunities should be researching places to find potential students or organizations they could get involved with.

The beauty of this strategy is that you will not only be able to find extremely relevant information, but you will also rapidly gain an understanding of who is doing this work in your area.

Most people will never bother to do this legwork.

As we have all experienced at some point, sitting around waiting for opportunities to come to us rarely works, and worse—it leaves our fate up to chance.

By implementing this strategy in your own career, you can fast-track yourself to breaking into any scene.

To help you on your research quest, I have a handy formula that you can use to help find what you're looking for.

This looks super simple and obvious, but I can't tell you how many people never think to try it.

Use this formula when searching on Google:

What you're looking for in *Your city*

OK, now let's talk specifics.

The following are meant to demonstrate possibilities of how to actually implement this strategy to do rigorous research in very little time.

Before we begin, I want to emphasize that these are examples to get you started.

I encourage you to think creatively for yourself and use these as a starting point.

Ready?

Let's go fishing.

Examples of fishing holes

Private teaching

Look up all of the local, regional, and state honor bands, jazz bands, orchestras, choirs, or anything along those lines, to identify which schools are placing students in those programs.

The schools that place a lot of students are likely worthwhile places to look for potential students because those programs clearly place an emphasis on music.

Do a quick Google search to locate the music schools around your area.

By reading their websites, see if you can get an idea where the students come from and who teaches them.

With some luck, you might even discover a place to find students that nobody else is teaching.

Do this for all levels and ages of students that you're interested in teaching.

Remember that every student playing in the high school honor ensembles came from a middle school, and probably another program before that.

Eventually, you will figure out how to get in touch with someone at these places that you think are worth reaching out to.

Follow the trail by browsing various websites.

It may be helpful to keep track of them so you can reference them later.

Church music

If you're a classical musician, then you are accustomed to playing church gigs of some kind.

To research opportunities with churches in your area, there are a few routes you could go.

While there are different traditions everywhere, the general strategies for research don't change.

Try searching for denominational listings of churches (*denomination of* church in *location*).

Results will obviously vary from area to area.

Even so, generally speaking, you will find something that acts as a hub of information for each area of beliefs.

This is another instance where a Google search can help you quickly find the information that you need.

Another option is to search for the closest chapters of organizations, such as the American Guild of Organists.

You will be amazed at how readily available this information is and how quickly you will become familiar with the places that have active music programs.

Holidays like Christmas and Easter are obvious candidates to quickly find a gig, especially if you are an organist or a brass player.

If you are in a busy area, these dates can be extremely difficult to book for the folks that are contracting, so don't be bashful about reaching out and saying hello.

Generally speaking, you want to reach out directly to the person who runs the church's music program.

If you can find any form of centralized information about the religious centers in your area, you will save yourself a ton of time.

Wedding music

Weddings are one of the few types of work out there that are relevant to just about any musician.

It doesn't matter if you are a string quartet looking to perform ceremonial music, a jazz trio trying to play for cocktail hours, or a drummer who wants to perform with local wedding bands.

There are fantastic resources at your disposal to find exactly what you're looking for.

Websites like weddingwire.com, theknot.com, and gigmasters.com (there are plenty of others too) have searchable listings of vendors based on genre and location.

These listings will show every group and performer that matches those results.

You can see which groups have the highest ratings and sometimes even who gets hired the most through that site.

This is invaluable information because it tells you exactly who is performing certain types of work, which you can then use to find the groups on Google.

If you're an individual, you can reach out directly to those groups about potentially working with them.

These sites also have the added benefit of allowing direct contact with wedding planners and venues, if you are a member of a group.

Feel free to get creative and explore the websites of various venues and planners because they could potentially be useful places to gather information as well.

Wedding scenes, especially in metropolitan areas, tend to be overcrowded.

Even so, don't let that deter you from researching and making a decision for yourself.

Later we will discuss how to time your outreach to people, but I want to be sure to point out that, like everything, weddings have busy and slow seasons.

Active ensembles

As an individual musician, one of the most important things you can do when you're just getting to know your local scene is to get a thorough understanding of what ensembles are in your area.

Depending on where you live, this can vary wildly; but having this knowledge will give you a solid idea of your options.

Aside from looking at sources similar to gigmasters.com, one of the best tools for research is through the local cultural alliance.

The names will differ from place to place, but essentially what you are looking for is a regional organization dedicated to promoting the local arts scene.

Virtually all of these organizations have directories of the ensembles in the area that can be searched and filtered to easily give you specific results.

Some quick searching online will likely lead you directly to this particular type of fishing hole.

Once you have located these directories (large cities might

have several), start bookmarking the websites for the relevant organizations.

You will be amazed at how much information is available through these types of directories, and you will rapidly gain insight to what options are in your area.

When browsing through these websites, I recommend you look for contact information for their personnel manager, contractor, orchestra manager, booking agent, or whoever seems like the most likely person to reach out to for hiring.

In addition to searching for the people responsible for hiring, I encourage you to browse through each group's rosters to get an idea of who the musicians are.

By doing this, you will better understand who is playing different types of gigs around town.

If you are not a classical musician, I recommend looking at local venue schedules to familiarize yourself with the groups performing in your particular space.

Regional colleges

If you are an orchestral musician or a vocalist, this might be an excellent opportunity to find freelance work.

When I was first getting started as a freelancer, I spent months trying to get creative about what type of gigs I could do.

As I mentioned before, one day I realized most of my work was subbing with colleges and universities with music departments that needed to complete their ensembles.

In this case, I found a Wikipedia article that listed all of the higher education institutions in my region, and I reached out to all of them.

By simply taking time to visit each site and locate contact information for the director of each ensemble, I was able to compile a list of almost every school and make contact in no time.

Within a few weeks of reaching out, I received a response back from nearly every school.

Years later, I have a great relationship with many of them.

All of those connections started with a cold email.

Don't be shy about reaching out to each ensemble's director because you never know when they might need someone.

Often each ensemble has their own budget, and they might do concerts where they hire extra musicians.

An example could be a choir hiring brass players to perform works with brass and choir.

While this particular fishing hole might not be relevant to you or your instrument, the main point is to be on the lookout for less obvious opportunities for your instrument.

I happened to stumble upon this great opportunity and knew that many ensembles often needed horn players.

Thus, I knew that I should be on the lookout for concerts that might need additional players.

Keep that opportunity mindset going at all times.

You never know, a gig might pop up when you least expect it.

Concert series

It doesn't matter if you play in a ska band or a string quartet, some of the best gigs out there can come from existing concert series.

There are a few ways to go about doing this research, but the easiest way is to go directly to performance calendars of similar groups.

By digging in the past, present, and future schedules of similar ensembles, you can immediately find out where potential opportunities lie.

By the way, if you just read that and thought something along the lines of *that feels like cheating*, I can assure you it's not.

You are simply looking for ideas at this point, and this is a great place to find them.

Generally speaking, once a group performs at a venue, they're probably not going to be back at the same venue immediately.

Even if they are, that's a reasonable sign that the venue is an excellent spot to play.

I want this to be as simple as possible for you to make progress, and this strategy will help you get there.

Concert series can take place anywhere from major concert halls to churches and bars.

With this research you can quickly get an idea what's out there, and by looking in these types of places, you will definitely find potential opportunities you never knew existed.

Action Step

Before you read any further, go ahead and take time to research various fishing holes.

Spend time digging around and take notes about what you find.

It won't take you long to start gaining an understanding of your local scene.

Write at least three potential fishing holes below:

_____

_____

_____

HOW TO GET A MENTOR

The power of mentors

"If I have seen further it is by standing on the shoulders of giants."

- Sir Isaac Newton

Some of the most influential relationships you will ever have will be with those who take you under their wings and invest time in you.

Anyone who is successful can tell you that their achievements would not have been possible without the guidance of mentors along the way.

Just like your teachers have helped you develop skills as a musician, there are tons of other people with skill sets you could benefit and learn from.

This applies to any area of life, not just freelancing as a musician.

If there is some aspect in your life that you want to improve, don't be shy about seeking advice from those you admire.

As I mentioned before, when I was finishing my degree, I was clueless about what I was going to do with my life after school.

There were several things I was interested in—teaching artistry, freelancing, private instruction, and business.

But there was only one problem.

I had very little experience in any of those things.

So, before I finished school, I decided to ask my teachers if they knew anyone who might be able to help me learn more about these interests.

After a few emails, some waiting around, and a lot of persistence, I ended up getting some responses.

A few of these people even ended up hiring me at some point over the next few years.

Just to give you some context of where I was starting, my only steady source of income was that job valeting cars at a hotel.

So here I was, a young musician with a valet job, a lot of debt, and no connections.

Once I began reaching out to everyone I could for advice, I slowly began to gain traction.

Within a few months, I had picked up a few private students from someone who was moving away, an unpaid internship with the Philadelphia Orchestra, and started relationships with several of the movers and shakers in various parts of the local scene.

I continued to follow this same process of reaching out to those who could offer some guidance.

Fast forward a few short years and I was the marketing manager for a local orchestra, had several positions as a teaching artist, and had a busy freelance schedule on the weekends.

This was an astronomical change that took place over a few short years.

All of this growth was made possible by constant curiosity to learn more and asking people I admired for help.

Now, this didn't just magically happen by sending a few of emails.

There were many people I reached out to who completely ignored me.

Even in those rejections, there were lessons to be learned.

More times than not, I sought mentorship in the wrong way.

It took a lot of trial and error to learn how to get amazing guidance from people way out of my league.

Next, I'll share with you the best tips I've learned about finding mentors.

10 rules for connecting with mentors

"Fools learn from experience. I prefer to learn from the experience of others."

-Otto von Bismarck

1. Reach out before you need help

When it comes to relationships, just like everything we have been talking about, you should always try to set yourself up for success down the road.

The worst time to first reach out to someone is when you are desperate for help.

Start researching people you admire now, and as you develop relationships over time, you will naturally know when it's OK to ask for something.

Always come from a place of trying to add value to them before making any requests of them.

2. Bring value to them

Be useful to them in any way you can.

This book has already covered how important it is to bring as much value as possible to others, but it's worth mentioning again.

If you're not sure what would be useful to people, try to identify the sources of stress in their life.

Do some research to quickly familiarize yourself with the types of activities they are involved in.

Learn as much as you can about them.

Try to find the places where you can make a meaningful contribution to them.

Even if you don't find the perfect thing that resonates with them, most people will appreciate the fact that you tried to offer help in some way.

3. Start from the bottom of the ladder

If you want to climb to the top, you're going to have to climb from the lower rungs first, right?

Everyone has a dream of getting to work with and learn from their idols.

The often untold truth, however, is that it can be extremely difficult to get into their circles if you are just starting out.

People at the top of their game tend to surround themselves with other high achievers.

If that's not you (yet), there is nothing to worry about.

When you're getting started, focus on connecting with others on your level instead of immediately shooting for the highest rungs.

It is exceptionally rare for newer players to get into those top positions with their idols, so don't be discouraged.

You will have much greater success by identifying the people who are more accessible to you at your current level.

Start by building rapport with those people on the lower rungs first.

Eventually, you will start to meet people on the next rung of the ladder, and you will continue working your way to the top from there.

4. Be ready to put in the time

The harsh truth is most people are lazy and don't want to invest time into anything or anyone.

If you want to get the most out of the connections you make, then you should be ready to absorb everything they've got to offer.

This means spend as much time with them as possible.

If they invite you to an event at 7am on a Saturday, then you need to show up.

If they recommend you read a book, read it and talk to them about your thoughts on what you read.

When people see that you're serious about learning from them and willing to put in the energy, they'll know that you're someone who is worth the investment of their valuable time.

5. Return the favors by making them look good

If you play your cards right, you may eventually find yourself caught up in a world you never thought accessible.

Great mentors can open doors to opportunities that you could never gain access to alone.

Whether it's access to their network, a job, or a reference for a great opportunity, once they trust you, they will start helping you out in some way.

With this in mind, know that the best way to repay your mentors is to do an amazing job on anything they've helped you gain access to.

Never make them regret recommending you for anything because how you perform is just as much a reflection on them as it is on you.

Always make your mentors feel great about investing in you, and the relationship will continue to grow over time.

6. Don't worry about the money

It is totally worth volunteering your time to get involved with a great mentor.

The time you put into the relationship is an investment into all of the knowledge you will gain from that person.

You know what works best in your financial situation, but don't lose sight of the long game and how what you learn now will benefit you throughout your entire career.

7. Be strategic with who you're reaching out to

Do research on anyone you are interested in meeting and learning from over time.

Make sure it's someone you like and admire.

Use your goals to guide your decisions as you seek help from those around you.

Try to identify people whose values align with yours and whose work excites you.

Those are the people you will likely click with and should aim to build a relationship with.

8. Manage your expectations of people

Don't create any kind of expectation of other people.

Anybody who is worth connecting with is probably successful in their own way.

Successful people are busy.

Respect their time and always be grateful for any time they offer you.

Remember, leave your entitlement at the door because nobody owes you anything.

9. Anyone can be a mentor

You don't have to know someone personally to have them as your mentor.

Over the years, I have learned a tremendous amount about life, business, and relationships from following my favorite authors, entrepreneurs, and musicians online.

Some of the most successful people in the world share their ideas for free every day through books, blogs, online courses, and podcasts.

There is a tremendous amount of information available to you, and if you proactively learn and act on what you learn, you'll be unstoppable.

You will be amazed at who you can connect with by reading their books and sending them an email that just says, "Hey, I read your book and implemented your ideas in my own life and got amazing results."

Hardly anyone actually follows through and sends these messages.

Put in the time to really understand the work of people you admire, and let them know you appreciate their work and have gotten a great deal of value from it.

Don't limit yourself to only the people physically around you.

Take action and start implementing good ideas you learn from anyone you can.

10. Don't ask them to be your mentor

This is simple and hopefully obvious, but don't ask anyone to be your mentor.

The word mentor is a scary word to a busy person—especially a busy person who has no clue who you are.

Follow these 10 guidelines to start cultivating a natural mentor relationship that will blossom over time.

Action Step

List three people you would love to be your mentors someday.

Remember, you're not going to ask them "Will you be my mentor?" Instead, start figuring out how to apply these 10 rules to reach out to each of them.

_____

_____

_____

SKILLS THAT HAVE NOTHING TO DO WITH TALENT

Basic freelancing skills

Some of the most important freelancing skills have nothing to do with how you play.

Yet, these skills will help lay the foundation of people's impressions of you.

It is striking how many professional musicians lack the organizational skills necessary to be dependable freelancers.

No matter how old you are, where you live, or what instrument you play, the skills in this section can become the most valuable assets of your professional life.

Instead of getting caught up worrying about things that don't really matter, focus your valuable time and energy on getting these things right, and you'll stand out from the pack.

Show up on time

I know, this sounds so obvious, and it is.

But it will amaze you how many people have difficulty with this.

A good general rule of thumb is to plan on arriving at least 15 minutes before call time.

The saying that being on time is actually late is a real thing and should be observed.

There's nothing worse than getting stuck in traffic, searching for a parking spot, then trying to figure out how to get on stage.

This is a situation where it is better to be safe than sorry.

I've been the guy who ran on stage just moments before a concert began because I got lost on the way and didn't know where to park.

It sucks to be that person.

It can make a horrible impression if everyone is stressed and worrying about whether you are going to arrive.

Trust me, if you're late people are going to know.

Check the traffic or transportation schedules before you leave and give yourself ample time to make sure you are on time for your commitments.

Keep a calendar

In the world of smartphones, there is no excuse for being unorganized.

Every possible device has some kind of calendar application on it.

Keep your calendar updated and always check it when asked about gigs.

You don't need fancy apps to stay organized.

Just use something that can keep track of your schedule and stick to it.

Double-booking yourself makes you look like you have no control over your time and reflects poorly on you.

Keep your commitments organized and use a calendar.

Be prepared for anything

The most seasoned freelancers seem to have everything they could possibly need tucked somewhere in their car.

As you start doing more work, you will better understand what things could go wrong and how to be prepared.

It's worth buying an extra music stand and bowtie to keep in your car.

Whatever tools are necessary for the work you are doing, try to keep them all in one accessible place.

Everyone will have the experience of forgetting their black socks at some point, so try to avoid this scenario by being the person who is prepared.

Communicate effectively

Imagine for a second that you are in charge of hiring an ensemble of 30 musicians for an upcoming gig.

You send out emails to everyone you know asking if they are available to play.

And then—half the people don't respond.

Did they get the email?

Are they unavailable?

Should you wait to hear back from them?

This is the life of a contractor; the truth is, it can be a major pain to deal with.

Remember when we talked about doing more work yourself and not creating more work for other people?

When you don't promptly reply to emails, you are essentially guaranteeing that the other person has to do more work.

That is the exact opposite of how it should be when you're trying to get work.

You should make other people's lives ridiculously easy by being a clear communicator.

Don't make them wait around and guess whether or not you are available.

If you need a couple days to confirm, just tell them that.

Simply acknowledging that you received their email is a giant step in the right direction.

You will make their life so much easier, which is always a good thing when trying to create business for yourself.

Dress appropriately

Don't show up looking sloppy.

Your appearance sends a signal to the world about who you are.

People's perceptions of you matter, so take an extra few minutes to look presentable.

You don't need to wear concert black to rehearsal, but you should always dress appropriately for your environment.

Offer to help

Being helpful to those around you is incredibly underappreciated in the world of freelancing.

The people behind the scenes are just as important (if not more so) than the performers on stage.

Don't make it a habit to have the *it's not my job* attitude.

If you see someone who could use a hand, just help the person out.

It could be something as simple as moving a few chairs around or collecting folders.

Be a team player and offer help to others when you can.

Don't be a whiner

Having a bad attitude is a quick way to kill the mood at a gig.

If you're having a crappy day, don't bring that along with you and spread it around.

Complaining is a waste of time in any situation, so just don't do it.

Nobody wants to sit next to someone who whines and complains about everything.

Chances are, if there really is something bad that warrants a comment, the other people already know.

Always keep a pleasant attitude and be the type of person you want to work with.

Be useful

"The best way to find yourself is to lose yourself in the service of others."

-Gandhi

Scott Adams, the creator of the megahit cartoon Dilbert, was once asked in an interview what he would put on a billboard if he had the freedom to write whatever he wanted.

His answer?

"Be useful."

What profound advice.

If you are truly useful to those around you, then you will be indispensable.

This might sound like weird advice for a book about freelancing, but it's extremely important to offer something valuable to those around you.

As we've discussed, value doesn't always have to be something with music.

The fastest way to be useful is to identify a problem, then create a solution.

Some of the most successful musicians I know have done this consistently throughout their careers.

This is the essence of entrepreneurship (which is what freelancing is in its own way).

Look for a problem that others are facing and solve it.

You read all about how to be valuable earlier in this book, and this is where you should start understanding how to put what you've learned into action.

Always be on the lookout for problems you could solve for others.

This could be literally anything.

I know many people that have amazing relationships with successful musicians they likely considered out of their league at some point.

They were able to establish a meaningful connection by doing things like:

- Babysitting during rehearsals
- Creating PDF versions of their sheet music
- Helping build a website
- Offering them a ride to a gig
- Operating a recorder or camera for a performance
- Transcribing music for their church band
- Watching their pets while they're on tour

These might seem like random things, and they are.

The point is that you should always be on the lookout for ways you can be useful to others.

Some things require unique skills, while some only require time and willingness to help out.

You will quickly find that people want to work with those who are useful to them.

Just remember, there will always be plenty of people who can play most gigs, but there will always be a demand for people who are useful in various ways.

HOW TO SELL (EVEN IF YOU HATE THE IDEA OF SELLING)

"Do one thing every day that scares you."

-Eleanor Roosevelt

Art of the soft sell

Nobody likes being sold something.

In fact, most people don't even like the word sell.

The truth is, the moment people sense that a person is selling them something, their guard goes up.

Most people seem to associate selling with the aggressive used car salesmen.

But that's not how you are going to learn to sell.

Actually, you will do the opposite.

One of the most effective tools you can have in your arsenal of skills is the ability to deliver a soft sell.

It's more comfortable for you, and it's more comfortable for them.

In a soft sell, your goal is to articulate the value of what you offer, and let your customers know they are in complete control of the final decision.

If you offer something of value to someone, and communicate that value effectively, you'll be much more successful when pitching people.

You never want to come across as pushy.

Instead, your goal is to be someone who has something relevant and valuable to offer others.

To give some context on what this looks like, below is the exact script I have used hundreds of times when reaching out to new people about the possibility of doing work for them.

You can adapt this for yourself by filling in your information in the underlined portions.

Hi _____,

My name is <u>your name</u>, and I'm a local <u>instrument you play</u>.

I just wanted to reach out and let you know that should you ever need <u>your service offering</u>, I'm available and would love to play.

I have performed with <u>group</u>, <u>group</u>, and <u>group</u> around the area and would to love the opportunity to work together sometime.

For your convenience, I've attached my <u>resume and/or recording/ website</u>.

Thanks for your time, and I hope to hear from you soon!

–Your name

VISIT BREAKINTOTHESCENE.COM/BONUSES
FOR A PDF VERSION OF THIS SCRIPT YOU CAN EASILY COPY AND PASTE FROM.

Here's the outline of this email and why it works:

1. **Friendly introduction:** Tell them exactly who you are and what you've got to offer.

2. **Provide value:** If you did your research prior to emailing them, this email won't seem random. They have a potential problem to solve, and you're providing a potential solution.

3. **Social proof:** By referencing your experience, you are sending the message that you are legitimate and have relevant experience. If you have a mutual connection with them, it never hurts to reference that connection as well. If you have worked with people they know, they are more likely to trust that you'll do a good job.

4. **Make it easy for them:** Give them everything they need in one place. Do the work for them by providing your recordings, resume, website, or whatever it is they need beyond your references to help establish credibility.

5. **Thank them for their time:** People are busy, and nobody wants more email. Make sure to thank them for their time and give a little nudge that you would like to connect.

That's it.

Emails like this are extremely easy to read and take less than a minute of the other person's time.

Never email someone a big block of text.

If your email looks like a lot of work to read, it has a slim chance of being read.

I can't tell you how many times people have emailed me asking for advice, a favor, or something else with a monster paragraph of text.

Just keep it short and simple.

That's the key to getting better results through your emails.

Some people will argue that you shouldn't reach out to people without their permission.

I understand where this argument comes from, but too many people take themselves out of the game by waiting for other people to come to them.

Of course, everyone already has their own list of contacts they like to use, and you should never imply that you could replace someone else.

The people who wait around for opportunities to come to them are going to waste a lot of time waiting for those emails to come in.

Don't be intimidated by the thought of reaching out to people you don't know.

As long as you're contacting them with something relevant and potentially valuable to them, you will be fine.

I know how scary the prospect of cold emailing people can be; but trust me, more people will appreciate your attempt to connect than you'd expect.

I've been the guy sitting at the computer deciding whether or not I should hit send on an email to someone I don't know.

Just remember this: If they don't know you exist, how will they hire you?

The early bird gets the gig

Do you ever feel like you're the absolute last person to know about every gig?

Forget about getting called for it, you might not have even known it existed.

This is extremely common among players that are just getting to know their scene.

I felt this way for several years.

Then one day a solution to this problem just clicked in my head.

If you're the first person to reach out about an opportunity, then you'll have a huge advantage over the people who are just waiting for the gig to come to them.

Armed with the research you did in the fishing holes section, figure out when your gig season begins and ends.

Once you understand this pattern, you can use it to your benefit to get a leg up on the freelancing calendar.

Some questions you should consider when researching are:

- Which ensembles could you play for in the area?
- When do their seasons begin?
- Are there specific weekends where many groups have performances that might require extra players?

As soon as you have the answers to these types of questions, use that knowledge and start reaching out to the ensembles in your area.

Timing is everything here, so make sure you stay in the loop with what's going on in the organizations you're interested in.

A good rule of thumb to follow is to make contact a few months before a potential gig.

If you don't get a response, wait a few weeks and try again.

Don't be a bother to them, but there's no harm in reaching out.

To put this in context, let's think about this from the perspective of most classically-based organizations.

The seasons typically begin in the fall and end in late spring, right?

Well, most organizations begin announcing their seasons during the spring and summer months, before the year programming begins in the fall.

Of course, the timeline varies in each situation, but, if you are the person paying attention and planning ahead, you are going to be way ahead of the game.

Be the first person in line and you will likely secure gigs just because you took the time to ask.

They're going to hire people, anyway.

Why shouldn't it be you?

Make it easy for them by reaching out first.

The year I started implementing this was the year I went from the musician who was lucky to pick up the scraps left by other freelancers in town, to a musician who was routinely getting calls for work.

You might find yourself getting regular calls for gigs just because they know that you are dependable and on top of things.

Being the first to initiate contact is a powerful, yet simple, strategy anyone can use.

If you make the decision to take matters into your own hands, you will reap the benefits for years to come.

Know your space

One thing you absolutely must have before you can sell your services is an intimate knowledge of the space you are working in.

People with a deep knowledge on a subject exude a confidence that cannot be faked.

If this isn't you (yet!), then you need to start learning the space any way you can.

If that means doing free work to build your experience, then go for it.

BREAK INTO THE SCENE

Completely immerse yourself in the books, music, concerts, and experiences that are necessary to learn as much as you can—then go out and implement it.

Until you know your space inside and out, you're going to be very limited in your options.

Just think, what good is a church musician who doesn't know the service music?

What about a woodwind doubler who wants to be on Broadway, but doesn't know the shows?

You must have the skills *and* knowledge to perform well.

If you're not there yet, don't sweat.

Just keep practicing.

The more experience you have, the more reliable you will be.

Having evidence that you can do the job before you get hired is enormously powerful.

People who are truly great at what they do can recognize others who also know what they're doing.

Likewise, they know when people are faking.

Becoming recognized as someone who knows what they're talking about gives you a certain authority that will set you apart from many other freelancers out there.

Understand their hopes, fears, and dreams

These are fundamental motivators behind any successful selling.

By appealing to the hopes, fears, or dreams of your customers (anyone who pays), you will be on the fast track to becoming a selling whiz.

There's a concept in the world of marketing known as *features vs. benefits*.

Features are just the tools that help get you to the goal, while benefits are the end result that people are really pursuing.

Let's imagine you are a private teacher.

A student, Suzie, comes to you for lessons.

She wants to start taking music more seriously, so she can make a career out of it.

What does Suzie truly care about?

It's not the lessons that she *really* cares about; it's the results from the lessons.

Suzie isn't paying to sit in a room for one hour each week.

That's not what she's after.

She is paying for the transformation in her musical abilities that are a result of private instruction.

Think about that for a moment because this is a significant point.

To illustrate this, let's pretend Suzie has the choice of two different teachers.

They're both equally qualified and have tons of experience.

On paper, they both seem like stellar candidates who could help Suzie reach her goal.

Teacher One talks to Suzie and focuses exclusively on the etudes, scale patterns, and solo works she will do during lessons.

After focusing on details, such as rates, location, and time, the call ends.

Several minutes later, Suzie calls Teacher Two and has a completely different conversation.

Instead of focusing on the details of what lessons will entail, Teacher Two takes time to really understand what Suzie is striving for.

This conversation is about what Suzie wants and how she can get there.

By recognizing that Suzie wants to become a professional musician, Teacher Two connects with Suzie on a more personal level than Teacher One.

If Teacher Two can demonstrate an understanding of what Suzie really cares about, then the choice is a no-brainer.

The difference between the two teachers is that one focused on the *features* of lessons, while the other focused on the *benefits* of lessons.

This approach will make your customer feel as though you understand their problems, and you are the only person who is going to solve them.

Once you grasp how to appeal to what other people are truly after, you will become the obvious choice in any situation where you have to sell to others.

Lead with why it matters to them

"Try not to become a man of success. Rather, become a man of value."

-Albert Einstein

When people are buying something, start the conversation with the thing that matters most to them.

With your new understanding of how to sell your ideas, put that into action by always leading with the benefit to the customer anytime you have to sell a product or service.

Start off every pitch with why it matters to them.

Don't talk about yourself; talk about the benefits for the customer.

To be honest, they probably don't care about you, but they do care about themselves.

You might be thinking, *that's such a negative way to look at it.*

Maybe that's true.

But at the end of the day, people pay for things that are valuable to them.

The faster you can articulate how your idea benefits them, the better off you will be.

Anytime you have an idea for a cool project that requires the help of others, you will need to sell it.

I am willing to bet that everyone reading this book has had at least one idea that really excited them.

Then they probably realized that you almost always need the cooperation of other people to make the idea a reality.

This is where people often get snagged.

When this happens to you, try to take a look at what the other person cares about.

It doesn't matter if you're a band trying to get a slot at the local bar, or if you're a string quartet trying to land a wedding gig.

The other person always cares about something, and it's your job to figure out how you can provide it, so they say "yes."

Make it easy for them to say "yes"

Anticipating objections before they come up is another essential part of the selling equation.

When you reach out to people, always try to be a few steps ahead of them.

They will almost certainly have objections, so you should be prepared to knock them out one at a time and still provide something of value.

If you're reading this, worrying that you have no idea what their objections will be, keep calm.

The more experience you get selling your ideas to others, the more familiar you will be with common objections and how to overcome them.

Each time you get turned down from something, make a note about what happened and why.

Look for patterns.

You will quickly gain awareness of the typical obstacles in your way.

The secret to making it easy for them to say "yes" is to remove as many barriers for them as possible.

Nobody wants to do more work.

When you ask other people for something, you are inherently creating more work for them.

Even if they have to stop what they're doing to do something for you, that's work.

It's time away from doing something else.

So, do your homework before you reach out to anyone.

Most people will find any excuse they can to get out of doing something extra.

Your job is to assume that they are incredibly busy and take any potential extra work off their plate.

Here's a scenario: let's say you're a jazz pianist, and you've got a trio that wants to pick up a few gigs at a local bar that has live music.

Before you ask about performing there, stop and think about all of the reasons they might have for why you can't play.

Then do your homework.

Check their schedule and find a night that is free.

Promise to bring your own gear (which means they have less work to do).

Tell them you will have an audience coming to hear you play, and then invite as many friends and family members as possible.

By doing these things, you found a night they potentially want entertainment; you assure them you will have your own gear; and most importantly of all, you will bring business to their establishment.

You can never guarantee results, but this will definitely get you a much better shot at landing the gig.

Go out of your way to make sure that the other person has to do as little work as possible.

Under promise and over deliver

I used to work for a very successful businessman named Frank.

Once in a while, I was privileged to sit and chat with him one-on-one.

One night, while sitting at the local jazz club, I asked about the best business advice anyone ever gave him.

As soon as I asked this question, he stopped for a moment, put down his drink, and leaned in.

He said, "Under promise and over deliver."

This idea is brilliant, especially when delivering a product or service to a customer.

At the end of the day, it's all about adding value, and one of the best things you can do is go beyond your customer's expectations.

Way too many musicians just show up to gigs at the exact time they're supposed to arrive and run out the door the moment the gig ends.

It doesn't take much to exceed the expectations of the person who hired you.

This could be something as simple as taking a request or sending a nice note afterward, thanking them for the opportunity.

Every gig is an opportunity for you to leave an exceptional impression on someone who could hire you again or recommend you to others.

Remember when my friends and I stayed out in the midst of a blizzard during an event?

That was going above and beyond the expectation, and it ultimately led to more opportunities.

There are very few people who will go out of their way to over deliver on what they promised.

Take every chance you get to bring more value than expected to those around you.

You will find that selling your skills or services becomes a lot easier because people will appreciate you and want to work with you.

Go for the low-hanging fruit

This is a widespread term in the world of professional sales, and it is equally applicable to freelance musicians.

Low-hanging fruit is basically the goals that require relatively little effort to reach.

Incorporate this thinking in your life, and it will help you make progress quickly.

Getting your first win as a freelancer has an enormous impact on validating your goals.

That first time someone pays you to make music is an amazing thing, and it's even better when it's an opportunity that you created yourself.

With this in mind, I encourage you to make it as a simple as possible to experience your first win.

Don't be afraid to go after the obvious gigs that are available for your instrument.

Singers can be section leaders in church choirs; string players can do weddings; guitarists can teach lessons anywhere.

The list goes on and on.

A great example that I have found to be true is if you are a brass player, there is absolutely no excuse for not having a gig on Easter

Sunday or Christmas Eve.

So, if you live in an area with a lot of churches, then these are essentially guaranteed work days.

And just because it's an obvious option doesn't make it any less of a gig.

If you have been following through on researching opportunities around your area for your instrument, then you should have a pretty good idea of how to get started securing these gigs.

Find those opportunities and immediately pursue them.

Before you know it, you will have a few gigs on your calendar.

How to reach out to anyone (and what to say)

When I speak on this topic, there is one question that is inevitable:

OK, this all sounds great, but what do I actually say?

There are two things that typically happen in this situation.

First, people get so overwhelmed by not knowing what to say that they never send an email.

At some point, we've all had to write an email and had no idea what to say.

After an absurd amount of time staring at the keyboard, we give up.

Before you know it, we close the window and never actually send the email.

This used to be pretty typical of me, so I know exactly how it feels.

The second thing that commonly happens is people ramble on forever, writing bulky paragraphs of text.

They write emails with so many words it is intimidating to even look at.

As a result, the email might not be read because it's just too much work for the other person.

I remember the first batch of emails I sent were a total bust.

I sent the same email to about 100 people and only received a handful of responses.

I had no clue why.

Take a look at the actual first email I sent trying to drum up gigs for my brass group.

Seth Hanes <hanes81@gmail.com>

Hi there!

My name is Seth Hanes and I am the horn player/manager for a brass quartet based here in Philadelphia that works all over the area. The group is made up of young professionals that have been trained at leading institutions around the country that include Julliard, Curtis Institute of Music, University of Michigan, and Temple University. We provide high quality music for a variety of occasions that include weddings, church services, and just about any event that requires music! Our rates are negotiable and vary depending on the occasion. In addition to this, our instrumentation is flexible and other instruments could be added or substituted!

For your convenience, I have attached a short sample of our playing to this email.

Thank you for your time and we hope to have the opportunity to meet and work with you in the future!

As you can see, I fell into the second common group of people.

I finally wrote something and pushed send, but I rambled.

Within a few hours, I did book our first gig.

But when I looked back at that email, I cringed.

I knew it could be better.

With a little patience, and a lot of trial and error, I eventually figured out one email script I could use over and over again that consistently got results.

I've found if you send a clear and concise email, you will dramatically improve the likelihood of getting the desired response.

This script will help you avoid the paralyzing feeling of not knowing what to say, and it will prevent you from those long-winded emails.

I know we already covered this, but it is so important that it's worth reviewing one more time.

Having a simple template will save you tons of time and headache, and most importantly, it will help you get started immediately.

Ready?

Just fill in the blanks.

Hi _____,

My name is <u>your name</u>, and I'm a local <u>instrument you play</u>.

I just wanted to reach out and let you know that should you ever *need <u>your service offering</u>, I'm available and would love to play.*

I have performed with <u>group</u>, <u>group</u> and <u>group</u> around the area and would to love the opportunity to work together sometime.

For your convenience, I've attached my <u>resume and/or recording/ website</u>.

Thanks for your time, and I hope to hear from you soon!

–Your name

> VISIT BREAKINTOTHESCENE.COM/BONUSES
> ***FOR A PDF VERSION OF THIS SCRIPT YOU CAN EASILY COPY AND PASTE FROM.***

You probably noticed this email is much cleaner and shorter than my first email.

It's easier to read and cuts the fluff.

Remember, you don't want to make more work or take more of their time than necessary.

Five sentences are plenty for an initial introduction email.

Do yourself (and anyone you reach out to) a favor and keep your message concise.

Are you ready to get started?

Gather all of the contacts you've collected and start reaching out to them.

Before you know it, you'll actually be connecting with people that could potentially hire you for years to come.

Action Step

Go to breakintothescene.com/bonuses and download the a PDF version of this script.

Use the email script to start contacting those you want to connect with.

Take time today and send a few emails.

Not later.

Not tomorrow.

Today.

The sooner you take action, the sooner you will take control of your career.

Use the template and get going.

MONEY FOR FREELANCERS

"We don't make movies to make money, we make money to make more movies."

-Walt Disney

How to know what to charge

The first time someone asks you what you charge can be intimidating, and maybe even a little confusing.

Many people panic because they are afraid they'll quote a price too high, and the potential client will walk away.

It may be tempting to lowball the price.

Instead, if you are not sure what to charge, the simplest way to learn is to ask other freelancers what they would charge for that type of gig.

It can be perplexing, but just know it's most important that you have the ability to deliver value proportionate to the price you charge.

There's a reason pop stars like Justin Timberlake and Taylor Swift can charge over one million dollars to perform at an event, while singer-songwriters can barely find places to play.

137

Justin Timberlake and Taylor Swift have audiences that will purchase tickets, merchandise, food, beverages, and ultimately, help those who hire them achieve their goals.

If you are a local singer-songwriter with no following, then it's a tougher sell to get them to hire you.

The establishment needs a crowd.

This is necessary to acknowledge in order to understand how your pricing should work.

The fees you can command for your services are directly related to the amount of value you bring the person hiring you.

When to work for free

Don't immediately write-off the idea of free work.

It can do wonders for your career.

Seriously.

I've gotten a lot of flak about my opinions on free work over the years, but I will explain my perspective of when free work can help you.

First off, let me explain the role it has played in my own life.

My entire career has been built on free work.

Everything I have ever been involved in originally stemmed from volunteering in some way, shape, or form.

When you start with no real experience in something, it can be incredibly frustrating when nobody will hire you because of that lack of experience.

I've been the guy who was denied countless time because I didn't have previous experience.

It was after experiencing this rejection time and time again that I decided to create my own experience and opportunities to learn.

By strategically selecting where I worked for free, I have been able to get started as a teaching artist, freelance horn player, web designer, marketing consultant, and even a speaker.

By strategic free work, I mean that there should be a specific reason to offer your service for free.

In my opinion, there are three kinds of free work worth doing.

Resume building

If you want to gain experience in a skill or a certain style of playing that you aren't comfortable with, then this is a great way to build your comfort with it.

If you have very little experience in certain situations, and want to learn something new, then it can be worth your time to take a gig for free.

The next time someone asks, "Have you played in a pit orchestra before?"

139

You can honestly say, "yes," even if you were not paid for that performance because now you have the experience.

Networking opportunities

Once in a while, there will be a volunteer ensemble performance where you might have the opportunity to meet someone special, who you might not otherwise have the opportunity to meet or perform with.

It could be anything from a benefit concert to a holiday caroling group.

The type of gig doesn't matter if it will allow you to sit next to people you'd like to meet.

Awesome experience

Just recently, I was invited to go on a free tour of China.

It wouldn't be a paid gig, but the trip would be an amazing experience.

Sometimes the experience gained is a good trade-off for doing a gig for free.

I've done many free gigs over the years that have led to many new opportunities that wouldn't have been possible without volunteering my time.

Managing cash flow

Money is a topic that most musicians hate to think about.

Trust me, I used to be that way too.

Money management can be an uncomfortable topic; and while I am certainly not a financial advisor, I want to address some of the common challenges that musicians face when it comes to keeping track of finances.

One of the biggest things everyone should know is that the income of freelancers can be wildly volatile.

There will be months when you feel awesome because of how many gigs you have, and other months when you have nothing.

Many musicians get to the end of spring, realize they have no work lined up for the summer, and aren't sure what they're going to do.

The best piece of advice I can give any freelance musician, especially a young one, is to plan ahead.

With that in mind, let's talk about a few ways to do that.

Again, I am not a financial advisor, but I can guarantee if you follow some of these principles, you will maintain financial responsibility no matter your level of income.

Avoid debt and aggressively pay it off

If you have student loan debt, don't worry because you're far from alone.

As someone who paid four years of out-of-state tuition, I can assure you of this.

The best thing you can do for yourself long-term is avoid acquiring more debt by all means necessary.

One of the worst decisions you can make is to turn to credit cards and loans to finance your life.

I'm awful at math and won't get into the details of how interest works, but just know that the amount of money you borrow from anywhere probably costs more than you think.

Interest on debt is no joke, and you should make sure that you understand the financial realities of the decisions you make about any type of debt or loan.

If you have debt, you should aggressively pay it off and get it out of your life.

Spending one afternoon focused on understanding your financial situation is a great first step to getting on a secure financial track.

It might suck.

To be honest, it probably will; but you (and your bank account) will thank you when that debt is paid off.

Live below your means

This seems so obvious, but it is shocking how many people live wildly beyond their means.

The best way to gain control over your finances is to make sure that you spend *less* than you earn.

Again, I know this sounds like a no-brainer, but it is part of our culture to live beyond our means.

Everyone wants a nicer apartment, a new car, and fancy clothes.

And you know what?

Me too!

But if you have inconsistent income or are just starting your career, do yourself a favor and live well below your means.

You never know when your car will breakdown or you'll have a surprise illness that requires an expensive visit to the doctor.

By living below your means, you give yourself the flexibility necessary to pay for these items as they come along.

If this means that you have to share an apartment with roommates, cook for yourself at home, and buy fewer new clothes, then so be it.

Spending less than you earn means you can save money in your busier freelancing months so that you have the cash reserves necessary to sustain your lifestyle in the lean months.

Save money every month

One of the best ways to lay a solid foundation of sustainable income over the long-term is consistently save money.

Too many people think that just because they don't make much money, they can't save.

Honestly, I think that's totally ridiculous and a lame excuse.

You don't have to save much money for it to make a difference.

Everyone can save a little bit each week or month.

It may seem insignificant, but even saving $50 each month goes a long way over time.

By simply setting aside that small amount each month, you'll save $600 each year.

After 10 years, you'll have saved $6,000 (not including any earned interest), which is awesome!

That could mean being able to pay for an unexpected car repair during a busy freelancing month.

Of course, you can make adjustments over time as your income fluctuates.

Seriously, just get started consistently saving, and you will be ahead of the game.

You might be thinking that you don't have any extra money to save.

I guarantee that you can get started saving money right away, and you will hardly miss such a small amount.

Seriously, you could save $50 by staying home for just one night instead of going out with friends to a bar.

Everyone can save something, and while it might not feel like much, over time it will make a huge difference in your finances.

Get a day job

I never understood why young musicians fight the idea of having a day job.

Having a day job doesn't make you less of a musician.

In fact, I think a day job can be incredibly valuable by giving you a steady income, a place to meet new people, and an opportunity to develop new skills.

There's absolutely nothing wrong with dog walking, babysitting, bartending, valeting, or working an office job.

Everyone loves to say that they won't have time to practice, teach, or freelance if they have a day job.

In rare cases, this might be true, but there are tons of jobs out there where you can earn a steady income and still designate time to your music.

If it will provide some stability and comfort in your life, then I think it's great to get a day job.

While it might take some time to find the right fit, it's worth pursuing because there is nothing quite like knowing that even in the months that you don't have any gigs, you won't have to stress about how to pay your bills.

BREAKING INTO THE SCENE

"One day at a time. It sounds so simple. It actually is simple but it isn't easy: it requires incredible support and fastidious structuring."

-Russell Brand

You already have everything you need to get started

Focus your time and energy on making the most of what you already have.

When you're first getting started, a fancy website, headshots, and a big network of connections are not necessities.

Direct your attention to things that you can control, and you will be in great shape.

Bring value to others

Your ability to provide value to those around you will be one of the biggest factors in determining your success as a freelancer.

It will help build an amazing network and make people want to connect with you.

Remember, the more valuable you are, the more people will want to be around you.

Maintain an opportunity mindset

Always be on the lookout for opportunities.

They are all around you, and it's your responsibility to find and take advantage of them.

If someone had told me that working in a parking garage after graduation would be a major stepping stone to where I am today, I would've thought they were crazy.

But looking back, I can clearly see how significant that job was to meeting the people who would eventually change my life.

You never know where opportunities will come from, so always view the world through the lens of the opportunity mindset.

Be proactive

Most people wait for things to happen to them.

You should do the opposite and be on the offense by being proactive and making things happen.

By always being proactive, you will take things into your own hands instead of waiting for them to happen to you.

People need to know you exist to hire you

One of the most common errors people make is operating under the assumption that other people know who you are.

If they haven't met you, there's a good chance they don't know you exist.

Don't be shy about reaching out to people using the scripts and strategies from this book.

Keep your goals in mind

Goals will help keep you on track.

It doesn't matter if they're large or small; have a destination in mind to help guide the actions you need to take to keep moving in the desired direction.

Remember, small wins are so important to build momentum, so don't be afraid to break your big goals down into smaller goals.

Create your own luck

The luckiest people out there are the ones who have been consistently positioning themselves in places where opportunities arise.

While you can't control luck, you can certainly influence the chances of good things happening to you by adding value to others, maintaining an opportunity mindset, and being proactive.

Don't just hope for something good to happen; put yourself out there and start creating your own luck.

Conquer those mental barriers

Mental barriers could be one of your biggest hurdles when you are getting started.

Often, the stories we tell ourselves are worse than what the actual outcomes will be.

Focus on taking action and pushing through this discomfort.

Connect with others

This book began by addressing the fact that building a career in music is a combination of talent and connections.

Building a strong network will be one of the most valuable things you can do as a musician.

Find the fishing holes and figure out how you can add as much value to those around you as possible.

The more positive relationships you have, the more opportunities will come your way.

Do the work

Put forth effort in order to make a change.

Don't just talk about it.

Don't complain about it.

Just decide you want things to be different and take action.

We live in an era that is unlike any other.

Take a moment to think about how much information you have access to.

BREAK INTO THE SCENE

You might be reading this on a tablet, computer, or smartphone.

You probably purchased this book from a website that allows you to order virtually anything and have it show up at your door within a couple of days.

There has never been another time like this, and if you want to make a change in your life, you must make the decision to take advantage of the opportunities around you and put in the effort.

Keep an open mind

Too many people count themselves out of the game before they even try to play it.

Don't pigeonhole yourself into believing that you can only do one thing.

That's total crap.

After you've invested a lot into something, it's easy to feel like you can't make a change and try something different.

It is never too late to switch things up and continue making adjustments as you go.

If someone had told me when I was in school that I would ever write a book, I would've thought they were crazy.

Careers can and should be fluid.

The fact that I get paid to learn how to build websites, market cool things that I'm interested in, and still get to play the horn professionally is an amazing thing.

Outside of playing the horn, none of these paths were even near my radar while I was in music school.

If I had maintained thinking that I had to pursue performing music full-time, I'm fairly certain I would be totally miserable right now—and this book never would have been written.

Follow through

If you have an idea for something that excites you, just do it.

Learn.

Fail.

Improve.

Most people rarely follow through on anything.

By developing the habit of being someone who follows through on things to completion, you will be more fulfilled and have much more value to offer the world around you.

This an unbelievably underappreciated skill by those who don't have it.

Having the ability to stick with things, even when they get tough, and see them all the way to completion will set you apart from the pack.

Anyone can talk about what they want to do, but very few have the discipline to stick to their guns and make things happen.

Start now

We talked about this earlier, but it is so important that I want to bring it back.

The future is uncertain, so don't wait around for the right time.

Nobody knows what will happen tomorrow.

Things can change in an instant.

If you don't start as soon as possible, you might never have the chance to do so.

Put it all together and start making things happen now.

Like many creative industries, the world of music is constantly plagued by talk of dwindling jobs and visions of the starving artist.

We work in an industry that is in desperate need of people that are ready to take change into their own hands.

Way too many musicians out there just want to show up, do the minimum amount of work, take the check, and go home.

There are only a handful of people in the music world who have that luxury.

The reality for most of us isn't like that.

Even in a space as crowded as music, it is shocking how much room there is for people who are willing to stand up and take control of their careers.

We can't all just assume that someone is going to raise the money, book the gigs, and market the performances that allow us to make a living.

The first step is to take personal accountability for your career.

My goal in writing this book was to help you start to carve your own career path.

I think you will quickly find that by following the hard-won advice in this book, you will start to see that it is possible to break into any scene.

With a lot of work and persistence, you can create the career you desire.

All right, I have one last request of you before you go off and start your adventure.

Can you share your experience with me?

After taking on this behemoth of a project, there is nothing I would love more than to hear from those of you who shared your attention with me and my work.

You can email me at seth@sethhanes.com.

I will read and respond to all the questions, comments, and concerns that come my way.

I am really psyched to see where you go.

Good luck!

ONE LAST THING

Will you do me a HUGE favor and review this book on Amazon. com?

Even a short review is greatly appreciated.

If you know a musician who is struggling to get started, I hope you'll consider sharing a copy of this book with them.

Also, don't forget to visit breakintothescene.com/bonuses to get free bonuses that can help you apply the material in the book and take the next steps that include:

- Exact scripts of the email templates you can copy and paste to use when reaching out to people
- A PDF version of my marketing course The Individual Musician's Guide to Authentically Marketing Themselves
- An exclusive resource list of my favorite books, articles, interviews, and more that you can use to help take your freelancing to the next level

And more, but you have to go to the site to find out what they are.

Thank you so much for reading and hopefully reviewing!

-Seth

ACKNOWLEDGEMENTS

It is absolutely amazing just how many people it takes to make a book happen.

There is no way I will be able to properly thank everyone that played a role in the develop of this book, but I will do my best.

First off, nobody deserves more recognition than my family.

Anyone who has ever lived with a young musician knows what a pain that can be, and my family not only dealt with it, but provided unwavering support in all of my endeavors since.

So, a huge thank you goes out to my parents, Brady and Teresa Hanes; my siblings and their families: Lacy, Jonathan (who asked to be included on an almost daily basis over the phone), and my niece, Elizabeth; my brother BJ and his family, Rachel, Porter (who is starting the cello), Evie Grace, Leah Kate; also, my sister Shea, and Steven.

Thanks for the constant support.

This book would not exist if it weren't for the incredible support from my writing coach, Azul.

Azul, thanks so much for helping me turn a total mess of thoughts into this book and guiding me through each step of the process to make this a successful project.

Also, thank you to my editor, Val Breit; Dane Low for the amazing cover design; and the whole Author's Writing Academy group for the constant support.

My amazing beta readers were an integral part of this project by generously providing feedback on this book before the rest of the world saw it:

Angela Beeching, Jason Heath, Rachel Shirley, Rachael Colman, Nick Pignataro, Nathan Fippinger, Joseph Bousso, Kate Amrine, Erin Morgan, Matthew Bauer, Jeremy Smith, Janos Sutyak, Natasha Jaffe, Philip Skabeikis, Amy Hearting, Kristina Bachrach, David Rosenfeld, Annii Lux, Lydia Roth, Jill Cathey, David Stevens, Matthew Valenzuela, Deb Spohnheimer, Sarah Younker, Kelly Brown, David Ciucevich, Mary Stahlhuth, Chris Herald, Byron Zeliotis, Derron Bell, Elizabeth Easley, Katherine Carleton, Mila Berry, Marie-Sonja Cotineau, April Ebeling, Laura Cricco-Lizza, Juanita Spicer, and Helena Feury (thanks cousin!)

Picking the cover of this book was a collaborative effort that wouldn't have been possible without the help of former teachers, family members, friends, blog readers, and so many others:

Alice-Lynn Stein, Alli Gessner, Andrew Hitz, Carolyn Tillstrom, Christopher Griffin, Chris Schelzi, Cody Roseboom, Dan Salera, Darian Evans, Darla Adams, David Ciucevich, David Kadavy, Dylan Younger, Emilie Patton, Eric Walker, Greg Stead, Holland Weaver, Isabel Escalante, Isaiah P., Jack Goff, Jack Kanoff, Jayden

Beaudoin, Jeremy E. Smith, Jessica Pollack, Jessica Smith, Joe Chen, Joel Deichman, Jonathan Wong, Jose Elias Alvarez, Joseph Bousso, Joy Mackey, Kat Guthrie, Katelain Tavares, Katherine Baloff, Kelly Brown, Kerry Morrison, Kristina Bachrach, Lauren Nowacki, Libby Ando, Madeline Bell, Mallory Sajewski, Mallory Tittle, Mark Meloon, Mary Stahlhuth, Matt Russell, Nat Eliason, Nick Thompson, Nina Swann, Perri Sussman, Rachael Colman, Rachel Kamradt, Ryan Everson, Stephen Silver, Susan Graham, Walter Barrett, my brother BJ, and my nephew Porter.

A special thanks to Eric Huckins and Gergana Haralampieva, who did the very first reading of this book before I made any edits.

I would have never gotten this far in the music business without the many incredible lessons I learned from my primary teachers over the years.

Thanks so much to Chris Griffin for showing me how to go big and introducing me to Philadelphia; and to Jeff Lang and Denise Tryon who taught me about life, music, and how to pass along what you know to others in a meaningful way.

One of the big topics of this book is about how to find and learn from great mentors.

I couldn't do acknowledgements without thanking the people that have made an enormous impact on my life in various ways.

Charlie Hoehn - Thanks so much for the infinite amount of generosity you have extended to me in the last year or so.

Through your books, courses, blog, and working together in various ways, I have learned a ton about being a good person from you.

David Kadavy - It's hilarious to think that we've only met in person one time, yet, I have gotten so much from you and your work.

You have given me so much valuable advice on everything from design and marketing to dealing with nightmare clients.

Thanks for being so generous, and I hope I have the opportunity to come down and hang out in Colombia very soon.

Frank Giordano - Thanks for taking a chance on an eager kid from your parking garage.

You probably regretted giving me your business card that day after I called you so many times, but I can't thank you enough for hearing me out, giving me my first job in marketing, and then encouraging me to strike out on my own.

I think about the advice from you that I shared in this book almost every day.

Mary Javian - I can't thank you enough for giving me a shot with so many different things over the years.

You have been incredibly supportive and generous since we initially met back in 2012.

Thanks for all teaching me so much and always giving me honest feedback when I need it.

And I owe a huge thanks to the entrepreneurs that I have been following for years who have provided endless inspiration, motivation, and help through your work: Tim Ferriss, Ramit Sethi, Ryan Holiday, Tim Grahl, James Altucher, Noah Kagan, Chase Jarvis, Seth Godin, and Gary Vaynerchuk.

I haven't had the opportunity to meet any of you yet, but I hope I get to thank you some day for all the help you've given me over the years.

But the final and most important acknowledgement of all must go out to you, my readers, for taking time to read this book.

This book would not exist without you.

ABOUT THE AUTHOR

Seth Hanes is a musician, digital marketing consultant, speaker, and founder of musiciansguidetohustling.com, which is regularly visited by musicians all over the world. He maintains a busy career as a performer and teacher around the Philadelphia area. As a digital marketing consultant, Seth has worked with everything from multi-million dollar organizations, book publishers, and musicians from ensembles like the Philadelphia Orchestra and the New York Philharmonic. In addition to his professional activities, he enjoys reading, learning to play the banjo, and spending time at the dog park with his dog, who is coincidentally named Banjo.

Seth can be reached by email at seth@sethhanes.com.
Say hello on any social media platform at @sethhanes

Made in the USA
San Bernardino, CA
24 January 2017